I0814627

— 150 —

WINE BARS

YOU NEED TO VISIT BEFORE — YOU DIE —

By Jurgen Lijcops

Lannoo

Introduction by Jurgen Lijcops

The best wine bars are a boon to humanity in many respects. Cosy, stylish and often inspiring locales where we can meet friends and relax. An inviting ambience – the final step in a creation process both natural and fascinating – forms the perfect setting for sophisticated drinks crafted in a symbiosis between terroir and winemaker.

As a sommelier with experience in a variety of restaurants and wine bars, I have always respectfully immersed myself in the collective endeavour that vineyards and winemakers embark upon to craft exceptional wine. In-depth courses, endless tastings, intense trainings, and continuous study. All are milestones on the journey taken by every professional sommelier. Relationships with gifted winemakers also serve as the basis for grasping the essence of making and serving wine. They afford insights into the finer points of the winemaking craft that cannot be gleaned from professional literature. Glimpses of the cherished, hard-won secrets of what makes some wines special and unique. This brings me to my mentor, the Flemish winemaker and pioneer Peter Colemont, owner of Clos d'Opleeuw, to whom I owe a debt of gratitude for honing and deepening my understanding of producing and assessing wines, and of the profession of sommelier.

With all of that knowledge, abundant experience, and professional connections in the wine world, selecting and assessing an authentic, exciting wine list becomes so much easier. Just as the excellence of the cuisine defines the quality of a restaurant, the skilfully selected wine references signal a wine bar's ambitions. And just as a restaurant's setting, interior, comfort and service levels are the DNA of its dining experience, location, views, décor, and hospitality are the essence of a truly unique wine bar.

In this book, you and I will travel the world, and visit 150 of the world’s most iconic wine bars. Stunning locales where tantalising and fascinating wine selections are served in an ambience that brings people together over an exquisite glass of wine.

In vino veritas!

OVERVIEW

AFRICA & THE MIDDLE EAST

THE AMERICAS

OVERVIEW

OVERVIEW

ASIA

OCEANIA

01 LA ROUTE DES VINS

72Q9+8RM, Impasse Bugeat, rue Paul Langevin, Abidjan, Ivory Coast

TO VISIT BEFORE YOU DIE BECAUSE

It's a champion of French organic wines and fine food, uniquely located in one of West Africa's booming metropolises

It's another wine miracle – here in tropical Ivory Coast, a beautiful country known for its fine cocoa beans and fresh ginger juice, you can also find some of the world's best natural wines and an abundance of the best French products. Initially opened by Franck Lainé in Togo in 2009, La Route des Vins relocated to Abidjan in 2017 and has been a hit with the locals ever since. Here guests can enjoy Lainé's hospitality along with a choice of 450 wines, from 150 mostly organic winemakers on the bar's lovely shady terrace. Favourites include Château de Fosse-Sèche, by sustainability champions Adrien and Guillaume Pire; Flo and Olivier Leriche's Domaine des Accoles and Olivier Bellanger's La Piffaudière. Also on offer are many great wines from Burgundy, Franck's native region. Guest sommeliers, such as John Euvrard, who has worked with Paul Bocuse for over 15 years, are regularly invited, while food includes charcuterie and cheese platters sourced from the best French producers.

la-route-des-vins-abidjan.business.site TEL +225 07 59 53 4498

02 13C BAR IN THE BACK

129 Arar St, Amman, Jordan

TO VISIT BEFORE YOU DIE BECAUSE

This chic bar, hidden behind the showroom of Jordan's leading wine producer, offers both world-class wines and food

Among the old souks and Roman ruins of Amman is a nondescript street that you must not miss: it is home to 13C Bar in the Back, one of the Middle East's top wine bars and restaurants. Named after the ideal temperature at which to store wine, it is accessed through a small door at the back of the fully stocked showroom of Jordan's Zumot Wines. A hidden oasis for wine lovers and foodies alike, it features Art Deco-inspired interiors, with a large oval bar and sheltered terrace. Any bottle of the 600 different wines from Jordan and Lebanon to the Mediterranean—including Zumot's very own Saint George Cabernet Sauvignon—can be bought from the shop and consumed in the bar for a minimal corkage fee. Its award-winning food offering focuses on Mediterranean small plates with Levantine touches, as well as a *risotto al vino* prepared with the diner's preferred wine, and a three-cheese mille-feuille that looks worth the trip to Jordan on its own.

13cwine.com; @barintheback TEL +962 7 9860 0616

03 L'APPARTEMENT

Jean Jalakh St, Achrafieh Sioufi, Beirut, Lebanon

TO VISIT
BEFORE YOU DIE
BECAUSE

Discover the lesser-known world of Lebanese wines in a secret oasis in the centre of bustling Beirut

'It all started in an apartment in Beirut where a group of friends and acquaintances would gather every week for an art atelier. We would paint, create and share stories over wine and music, always leaving feeling more connected and inspired than before,' explains L'Appartement's founding team. The gathering grew in popularity, and a new wine bar and bistro was born, first as an underground speakeasy, and now as a terrace in a hidden garden in the heart of Beirut. Its focus is on Lebanese wines—the country has a rich history dating back thousands of years. Its unique geography and climate provide ideal conditions for growing a number of grape varietals, resulting in rich and complex flavours, from crisp whites to bold reds. On the constantly growing menu are bottles of Ixsir, Château Qanafar, Terre Joie, Vignoble Joura, Château Khoury and Château Nakad, while foodwise you can expect French dishes such as *steak frites* and *pain perdu*.

@lappartementbeirut TEL +961 3 343 076

The Bar at Nile Plaza

04 THE BAR AT NILE PLAZA

1089 Corniche El Nil, 11519 Garden City, Cairo, Egypt

TO VISIT BEFORE YOU DIE BECAUSE

This chic hotel bar overlooking the mighty Nile is the place to sample the hidden gems that are Egyptian wines

Although Egypt is not widely known for its winemaking tradition, it actually has a pretty impressive one. It dates back to the 3rd millennium BCE, when a thriving industry was established in the Nile Delta to supply the red wine that played a key role in ancient Egypt's ceremonial life. Today there are still a handful of producers in the country, and one of the best places to sample their wines is The Bar at Four Seasons Cairo at Nile Plaza. With wonderful views over Cairo and the Nile, this plush third-floor bar is decorated with Art Deco motifs and classy portraits of Egyptian movie stars from the 1940s and 1950s by leading local studio photographer Van Leo. Head bartender Hany Moussa's 'By the Glass' menu offers a selection of Egypt's sparkling, rosé, white and red wines, from the Nile Vineyards' Lavita Secco to Gianaclis Vineyards' Omar Khayyam Sultanine Blanche/Bobal. Other local winemakers featured include Karm El Nada Vineyards and Egybev's Beausoleil. Bar snacks include a hit list of world dishes, including a large selection of sushi.

fourseasons.com/caironp

TEL +20 2 27917000

05 CULTURE

103 Bree St, Cape Town City Centre, Cape Town
8001, South Africa

TO VISIT
BEFORE YOU DIE
BECAUSE

This award-winning wine bar offers a carefully curated selection of all-time classics and unusual bottles

Opened in 2020 on Cape Town's coolest block, Culture is a buzzing wine bar with warm and inviting interiors by Stokperd. The key to it success is its offer of over 45 wines by the glass, from a diverse wine list, which owner Matt Manning has put a 'great deal of time, love and effort into curating'. Choose from two award-wining menus that blend quirky and well-known wines: the Culture List focuses on local wines including Mullineux Chenin Blanc 2020, Sons of Sugarland Barbera and Graham Beck Blanc de Blancs; while the Wanderlist, a collaboration with Radford Dale Imports, features international wines such as Yalumba Y Series Riesling, Yves Cuilleron Les Vignes d'à Côté and Jean Chartron Rully. In addition to the traditional cheese and charcuterie boards, tapas options include delicious tempura broccoli and beef shin croquettes. Just above the bar is the Wine Library, a members' club with a walk-in cellar and a hub for South Africa's leading wine professionals.

culturewinebar.com TEL +27 87 153 5246

06 LEO'S

Shop 28, De Oude Schuur, 120 Bree St, Cape Town 8001, South Africa

TO VISIT BEFORE YOU DIE BECAUSE

It's small but perfectly formed, offering not only an exciting selection of wines, but also great food and art

Another Bree Street stalwart is this little family business, Max's bagel shop by day, and Leo's wine bar by night—a truly unusual but delicious combo. It's known for its pizza bagels and food pop-ups (think ramens, fish burgers and Spanish tapas) prepared by top chefs from South Africa and beyond. But the main draw is its selection of low-intervention wines and ciders from small producers. On the menu are bottles such as Force Celeste Chenin Blanc, Testalonga El Bandito, Whole Bunch Syrah and Craven Pinot Gris. The team loves nothing more than tasting the latest 'bonkers co-ferment' and selecting wines that 'challenge and surprise'. Co-owner Matthew Freemantle's love for collaborations and art means plenty of exciting projects, from producing its own Fun Cat rosé, to artworks on the walls curated by designer friends Hoick Studios. (Past exhibitions include a series of monotypes inspired by outtakes of overheard bar chatter.)

leoswinebar.com TEL +27 76 042 0224

07 PUBLIK WINE BAR

1d Kloof Nek Rd, Tamboerskloof,
Cape Town 8001, South Africa

TO VISIT
BEFORE YOU DIE
BECAUSE

This bar is on a mission 'to turn wine upside down', showcasing the best of artisan and sustainable South African wines

Located a stone's throw from the Iziko South African Gallery, this trendy neighbourhood wine bar focuses on new-wave, alternative wines made by a talented bunch of South African winemakers, many of whom follow organic, biodynamic or natural production methods. Unpretentious and accessible, it's the perfect place to discover lesser-known gems, 'honest wines made from sustainably farmed vineyards and with minimal intervention in the cellar'. Thanks to its daily changing by-the-glass list and around 100 wines by the bottle, you can enjoy labels such as Savage Wines, Alheit Vineyards, Crystallum, Mullineux, Tim Hillock and Sadie Family (as well as a few like-minded European winemakers), while listening to a great playlist. Sampling chef Andrew's delicious fare is also a must; the tempting menu includes cannelloni, 24-month-aged prosciutto, house-made pickles, burrata and anchovies. Pop-ups by local restaurateurs such as Mulberry & Prince complete the ever-changing offer, which is definitely worth repeat visits.

publik.co.za

TEL +27 82 000 0000

08 THE AGENCY DUBAI

Lobby Level, Jumeirah Emirates Tower, Dubai, United Arab Emirates

TO VISIT BEFORE YOU DIE BECAUSE

Plush vintage-inspired interiors provide the perfect setting to savour a great selection of wines

A stalwart of Dubai's wine scene for decades, The Agency has recently reopened in the Jumeirah Emirates Towers with a glamorous new look of dark wood panelling, mirrored walls and crushed velvet booths. Its walk-in wine fridge showcases over 200 wine labels, one of the largest selections in town, while its expertise lies primarily in old-world wines, particularly those from Italy and France, with star items including Italian Amarone della Velpolicella, Brunellos and Chiantis, and French Châteauneuf-du-Pape, Côte de Nuits, Georges Duboeuf and Chateau Les Combes. Wine by the glass include Argentine Malbecs and South African Syrahs, as well as Sauvignon Blanc from California and New Zealand and a Pech-Latt Corbières rosé. There's also a great selection of cheese and cold cuts, including a generous platter for two that includes bresaola, smoked duck, truffle brie and marinated feta. Tucked behind the bar is a hidden cigar lounge.

jumeirah.com/en/dine/dubai/emirates-the-agency

TEL +971 4 330 0000

09 CAVE DUBAI

Sheikh Zayed Road, Mezzanine 2, Dubai, United Arab Emirates

TO VISIT BEFORE YOU DIE BECAUSE

This atmospheric cellar-inspired bar offers some of the finest wines from around the world

Standing in striking contrast to the city's bright glass skyscrapers, this dark and moody wine cellar is located in the heart of the five-star Conrad Dubai. Featuring beautifully lit wine bottles and walls, brown leather banquettes and a plethora of wine corks, as well as some fireside seating, it's a cosy place and the perfect spot to enjoy a selection of 1,500 international wines, one of the largest bubbly and grape selections in Dubai. A beautifully balanced list of champagnes, vintage, non-vintage and award-winning wines changes each season, while the eclectic range of premium wines by the glass features the likes of Dr Loosen Riesling from Germany and Marius by Michel Chapoutier Cinsault-Grenache from France. It is matched with a Parisian-inspired menu offering dishes such as duck rillettes, *tartes flambées* and profiteroles. There's also a Grape Tasting Experience by in-house sommelier Mariana Campos, a 'straight from the barrel' experience, and a private dining room in a striking wine cellar.

conraddubaihotel.com/dine TEL +971 4 444 7444

10 GRAPESKIN

Al Multaqa St, La Ville Hotel & Suites City Walk,
Dubai, United Arab Emirates

TO VISIT
BEFORE YOU DIE
BECAUSE

It's the ideal place for a spot of 'bottled poetry' and some delightful wine and cheese pairings

A bright open space with industrial furnishings and a charming courtyard terrace, Grapeskin offers wines to suit any mood. On the wine menu a set of designed emojis such as 'feeling gorgeous', 'ready to party' and 'hungry & thirsty' helps you pair a wine to your mood, with the help of the bar's expert sommeliers. It might sound a bit of a gimmick but it really works, thanks in part to a choice of more than 40 types of wine by the glass, as well as an ever-changing 'wine of the week' collection featuring bottles from vineyards around the world, including Greece, India, Italy and South Africa. Not to be missed are the Grape & Cheese Discovery menu, where you can try a port from Douro with blue cheese or a Freixenet Cava with sheep's cheese, and the monthly Wine Maker evenings, which invite wine enthusiasts to meet vineyard owners and wine producers from all corners of the globe.

livelaville.com/dining/grapeskin TEL +971 4 403 3111

11 MR PANTS WINE BAR

Shop 7, Delta Central, 74 Hillcrest Ave, Blairgowrie, Randburg 2194, South Africa

TO VISIT BEFORE YOU DIE BECAUSE

If you love wine but hate pomp and ceremony, this beautifully stocked and super-friendly bar is a real corker

There's no dress code here at Shayne Holt's Mr Pants—just wear your comfiest shorts and sandals, sit down, have a chat with one of the regulars and enjoy the ride. It's a tiny place, with only a 15m² room and a team of three behind the bar, but it does have a wonderful, spacious terrace, and offers over 100 wines by the glass, preserved using Coravin and sold with low mark-ups. Although there is no particular focus on specific wines, the menu includes bottles from every major region around the world (including first-growth Bordeaux, grand cru Burgundy and top-tier Barolo), with a predilection for smaller producers and the team's latest discoveries. Holt, who qualified as a sommelier in 2019 and since then has only wanted to 'taste, taste, taste', is particularly fond of Chablis, Mosel Riesling and Barolo. Although the cosy décor was planned on a shoestring, all the other wine-related essentials are high spec, from the bar snacks to the fridge and stemware. And to top it all off, Holt also owns a pizza place around the corner called Coalition Pizza, which delivers to your table.

mrpantswine.co.za TEL +27 67 294 1673

12 PROUD MARY

The Bank, 26 Cradock Ave, Rosebank, Johannesburg 2196, South Africa

TO VISIT BEFORE YOU DIE BECAUSE

A wonderful selection of South African wines, served at a stunning bar counter in the heart of cosmopolitan Rosebank

Proud Mary certainly knows how to make an impression, with its bold, mid-century modern interiors designed by Enrike de Wet of Sketch Studio, and colourful art selection on the walls curated by Morné Visagie. But it's definitely not a case of style over substance: the wine list celebrates small-batch, local and independent wineries showcasing a host of exemplary and unusual wines. Among its selection of South African winemakers are Pieter Ferreira and Van Loggerenberg Geronimo from Stellenbosch, and Carinus Family Vineyards from Swartland, the Lourens Family from Western Cape and Restless River from Upper Hemel-an-Aarde. Also on the menu is a generous list of champagnes and international wines, including French classics by the likes of Moët & Chandon and Louis Roederer, as well as local sparkling wines including the excellently named Testalonga 'I Wish I Was A Ninja' Pet Nat 480. Proud Mary is also a restaurant, serving beautifully presented dishes such as Cape Malay curry and seafood linguine, as well as a delicious *crème brûlée* cheesecake.

proudmary.co.za TEL +27 10 023 3316

13 VINÓFILOS TRIANA

C. Viera y Clavijo, 23, 35002 Las Palmas de Gran Canaria, Las Palmas, Spain

TO VISIT BEFORE YOU DIE BECAUSE

It's a delightful spot to sample some local wine and food, and discover a great selection of Spanish bottles

Easily spotted from the street thanks to its wonderful tiled façade and bright blue doors, this wine store and bar was opened in 2019 by local wine distributor Vinófilos in Las Palmas' historic centre. There are over 70 different wines available to drink by the glass, in a monthly selection that includes cavas, champagnes, Glou Glou vermouths and fine Jerez wines. The shop also stocks more than 1,500 bottles from all over the world, available to try with a corkage fee, and easily paired with some first-class tapas. These include a selection of local cheese as well as the Canarian classic *papas arrugadas con mojos* (wrinkled potatoes with dips). It is also the place to discover the Canary Islands' wine production, from a Tajinaste Blanco Seco from La Orotava in Tenerife to a Mondalón Rosado rosé from Gran Canaria. There is also a tasting room where the team holds introductory wine courses, pairing workshops and tastings on specific grape varieties, wine-growing areas or vintages of the same wine.

vinofilos.es TEL +34 828 07 16 56

14 SPEK & BONE

84 Dorp St, Stellenbosch Central, Stellenbosch 7600, South Africa

TO VISIT BEFORE YOU DIE BECAUSE

Celebrity chef Bertus Basson's wine bar is set in a historic townhouse in the heart of South Africa's wine country

Tucked away next to the old Stellenbosch market, the award-winning wine bar Spek & Bone is named after chef Basson's pet pig and puppy, 'who are (surprisingly) best friends and truly inseparable'. The pets themselves were named after the classic food combination of pork and beans, reflecting the bar's search for authentic simplicity. Here, you can sit under the oldest fruit-producing vine in Stellenbosch and enjoy a tapas menu 'with big, bold flavours' paired with specially selected South African wines. Among the favourites on the food menu are the Korean fried chicken and gnocchi with mushrooms and provolone, while the wine menu zooms in on boutique, small-batch wines with an interesting story. These include Thorne and Daughters' Snakes and Ladders Sauvignon Blanc, named after the highs and lows of growing vines high up in the Citrusdal Mountain; Julien Schaal 'Born of Fire' Chenin Blanc, and Minimalist 'Stars in the Dark' Syrah. Also worth a try is Basson & Son's very own Spek Red Blend (Kaapzicht Estate Blend).

bertusbasson.com TEL +27 82 569 8958

15 BARTINNEY WINE & CHAMPAGNE BAR

5 Bird St, Stellenbosch, Cape Town 7600, South Africa

TO VISIT BEFORE YOU DIE BECAUSE

Where best to celebrate Stellenbosch's 364-year-old winemaking tradition than in the oldest wine bar in town?

An Old World space in a New World wine country, this historic wine and champagne bar is housed in Stellenbosch's first bank, and today you can still see original features such as the Robben Island slate tiles on the veranda and the wooden front of the bank manager's office. It belongs to the Bartinney Wine Estate, located in the mountainous vineyards above Stellenbosch, and focuses on its award-winning Chardonnay and Cabernet Sauvignon. Sit on antique chair by the fireplace, or on the shady terrace, and enjoy a glass of sustainably produced Premium Hourglass Chardonnay and Skyfall Cabernet Sauvignon, or a glass of Grand Brut Cap Classique from sibling estate Plaisir Wine. All these wines are paired with locally produced, artisan-made cheeses and charcuterie. A multisensory tasting allows you to taste the three estate wines alongside fynbos, the native scrubland plants grown on the farm. Still thirsty? Next door is the Plaisir Wine & Gin Lounge, an elegant space serving wine and gin cocktails.

bartinney.co.za

TEL +27 76 348 5374

16 THE WINE GLASS

13 Ryneveld St, Stellenbosch 7600, South Africa

TO VISIT BEFORE YOU DIE BECAUSE

Sample the best of Stellenbosch's wines on the welcoming terrace, then stay on for a delicious lunch or dinner

Located in the heart of historic Stellenbosch, The Wine Glass is a bright and airy spot that serves 130 local wines by the glass and offers great tasting sessions. All the wines of the region are available in tasting flights of six glasses, a popular experience which comes complete with a set of tasting notes, pencil and spittoons, all ready for a spot of show and tell by one of the team's expert sommeliers. Flights can be specific: by cultivar (such as Cap Classique) or in overview—a combined flight of either red or white to showcase specific wines of the area. The Chardonnay tasting, for example, includes two Kleine Zalze, a Glenelly Glass, a Louisvale Chavant, a Hartenberg and a Longridge. Nibbles include fresh Atlantic oysters and large cold platters, while the restaurant also serves more substantial dishes such as the signature fillet of beef with coriander and the harissa-fried prawns. The Wine Glass is clearly on to something: it also has a busy outpost in Hermanus and the owners are planning to expand to Johannesburg and Cape Town.

thewineglass.guru TEL +27 82 555 2332

17 BRUT

36 Nahalat Binyamin St, Tel Aviv-Yafo, Israel

TO VISIT
BEFORE YOU DIE
BECAUSE

This gem of a bistro in bustling Tel Aviv celebrates the best of the local terroir, with both wines and cutting-edge dishes

Located in the centre of Tel Aviv, this small wine bistro is the passion project of talented pair Yair Yosefi and Omer Ben-Gal. Its extensive wine list of 200 labels is at once a love letter to all things French and Italian, while also championing Israel's emerging winemakers. The owners work with Israeli wineries–including Ya'acov Oryah, Bar-Maor, Abaya, Harashim and Agur–on blends that are grown and bottled exclusively for Brut, and aim to celebrate the local terroir, culture and communities. On top of this, they also import distinctive European wines from small-scale producers in Bourgogne and Piedmont. Brut is also celebrated for its ever-shifting, always exciting selection of seasonal dishes that reflect the duo's love for all things French and Italian, but stay rooted in local Middle Eastern tradition, using ingredients such as lamb and yogurt from Nazareth and vegetables from Hebron. Their interpretation of local culinary traditions, especially the Palestinian one which is a big influence on their work, is always thoughtful and perfectly balanced.

brutwinebar.com

TEL +972 3 510 2923

18 BOSSER

5 HaHashmal St, Tel Aviv-Yafo, Israel

TO VISIT
BEFORE YOU DIE
BECAUSE

Bosser's passionate team curates an excellent list of Old World wines in a relaxed setting in trendy Tel Aviv

Bosser is proof that at least one positive emerged from the pandemic years. It opened in Tel Aviv during the COVID-19 pandemic, when wine stores were one of the few businesses allowed to open their doors. A way to help small importers sell their wines while eateries were shut, the bottle shop turned into a full-blown bar as soon as it was safe to do so. Now it has over 200 labels on offer, mostly from micro-importers and boutique wineries from the Old World, handpicked by the team after research trips to France and beyond. (The owners are particularly keen on Burgundy wines and natural wines.) Not only does it have a great atmosphere, but some great snacks too. In winter you can pair a fresh Riesling with a homemade choucroute or a Portuguese Albariño with stuffed cabbage rolls, but otherwise, food is kept simple—marinated olives, cheese plates and bruschettas—to let the wines shine. Watch out for special tastings and culinary pop-ups by the likes of the Cantor sisters.

@bosserwines TEL +972 54 727 3443

19 CAVA WINE

Carrera 6 #67-63, Bogotá, Columbia

TO VISIT BEFORE YOU DIE BECAUSE

You can sit back and relax in this cosy wine lounge that offers a great selection of wines from around the world at affordable prices

Childhood friends Valeria Covo and Juliana Lecompte grew up together in Cartagena and share a passion for both great wines and lounging about on a nice plump sofa. It was while enjoying both of these at a friend's house that they realised what was missing from Bogotá's wine scene: a comfy bar with nice couches on which to enjoy a good wine at a reasonable price. They set about putting this right, opening Cava Wine in 2018 in the Colombian capital's charming Zona G, also known as Zona Gourmet. Designed as a welcoming living room, the space features Spanish tiles, vintage custom-made windows, wooden floors and sofas. The team of sommeliers will guide you through the bar's wine library, which stocks wines such as Zorzal Eggo Franco Cabernet Franc, Heinrich Blaufränkisch and Louis Latour Chablis. Tastings are held on Thursdays and Saturdays, while food specialities include truffled burrata pizza and baked brie. The bar is also a deli and bottle shop with over 400 references, and it delivers, so customers can enjoy their bottles on their own sofa at home.

cava.com.co

TEL +57 321 3037885

20 HALEY.HENRY

45 Province St, Boston, MA 02108, USA

TO VISIT
BEFORE YOU DIE
BECAUSE

Expert sommelier Haley Fortier's Boston bar is known both for its award-winning wine list and party atmosphere

A homage to Boston's maritime setting, this fun little bar looks to the ocean for both style and sustenance: the space is ship-shape with nautical details that make you feel like you are in the galley of a big ship, while the menu features all sorts of quality tinned fish. Opened in 2016 by Haley Fortier, the bar was very quickly recognised for its excellent wine list, which made it to the James Beard shortlist, not once, but twice. Described as a 'fun and flirty hospitality with a wine programme focusing on natural, sustainable and responsibly made wine from around the globe', the bar offers around 70 wines, available as half-bottle, in a daily changing menu of small-batch wines including Australian Slow Poke Pinot Gris and Hausherr's Jardin La Haut Riesling and Gewürztraminer blend. House specials are the haley henry mackerel in piri-piri sauce, served with fresh locally made rolls, butter, herbs and lemon, and the Muva beef sliders with a secret steak sauce. The tight-knit crew is passionate about wine–as well as 1990s hip-hop apparently–and make sure everyone is welcomed aboard. High tides, good vibes.

haleyhenry.com TEL +1 617 208 6000

21 PAIN ET VIN

Gorriti 5132, C1414 BJT, Buenos Aires, Argentina

TO VISIT
BEFORE YOU DIE
BECAUSE

A real labour of love, this little gem caters to all oenophiles and gourmets, with a focus on Argentinian wines

When Argentinian sommelier Eleonora Jezzi met Israeli chef Ohad Weiner, it was a match in heaven. Not only have they produced two wonderful children, but their other baby is this lovely wine bar near Buenos Aires' Plaza Serrano, the bohemian heart of the Palermo Soho neighbourhood. When it opened in 2013, it was one of the first of the new wine bars in town. It is still going strong today, thanks to the couple's enthusiasm and laid-back attitude. 'We love to travel and visit as many wine bars as we can, and we always prefer the cosy ones,' says Jezzi. 'That was a must when we began planning ours. The premise is that, no matter how much you know about wines, we have something we love to offer, and there's a reason for every bottle to be there.' The menu caters to all tastes, from natural wines to classics, while wine flights focus on themes such as great Argentinian whites, Malbec Terroir or Low Intervention. Last but not least, Weiner's delicious dishes are inspired by his Mediterranean roots and extensive travels, from fish kebab pita to smoked aubergine with miso and peanuts.

pain-et-vin.com

TEL +54 11 4832-5654

22 SOLERA ALMACÉN DE VINOS Y TAPAS

Eugenio Sainz Martínez esquina Ruta 10, José Ignacio, Maldonado, Uruguay

TO VISIT BEFORE YOU DIE BECAUSE

This welcoming seaside wine bar is absolute perfection and the highlight of many a visit to Uruguay

Located in the fashionable Uruguayan seaside resort of José Ignocio, Solera is packed all through the summer season, and with good reason. Its selection of wines is 60 per cent Uruguayan (leading local winemakers include Bodega Garzón, Santa Rosa and Carrau) but also include Argentinian, Chilean and Old World (mostly Spanish) bottles. Sommelier, owner and perfect hostess Soledad Bassini is in charge of a 350-label-strong list, while her partner, Fernando, is behind the bar's hand-built industrial boho décor, designed to make everyone feel at home. The top-selling wines are mostly rosés from Uruguay to Provence and Tannat, Uruguay's national grape, but Pinot Noir and some light red varieties are also very popular. The tapas menu features fresh and seasonal Uruguayan ingredients, and the matured rare beef tenderloin, raw fish tiradito and Basque-style cheesecake are particular favourites. Solera is also a bottle shop and sells wine to go all year round, so whatever the season, make sure you stop by if you are lucky enough to be in the area.

@soleravinosytapas TEL +598 98 869 372

23 HAY PAN

Calle Murillo 764, La Paz, Bolivia

TO VISIT BEFORE YOU DIE BECAUSE

Discover the highlights of Bolivian wine production in the world's highest capital

Hiding in plain sight in touristy central La Paz is this cosy little spot dedicated to Bolivian wines. The chaotic and colourful capital is actually at the centre of a blossoming wine scene, and there's no better introduction than Hay Pan, which was founded only a few years ago by Sukko Stach, Camila Zerda and Alfredo Montecinos. Named after the sign 'We have bread' often seen at local corner shops, it offers an excellent wine list featuring lots of small local producers. It includes 'white wine from the Valle de Cinti, a variety called Negra Criolla that currently can only be tasted in Bolivia due to its low production, as well as our emblematic white wine from the Marquez de la Vina Winery, which is made with Moscatel from the Luribay valleys,' explains Alberto. Other highlights include red and rosé wines from the Cinti Valley; platters of *piqueos* (appetisers) such as mini *empañadas* and juicy brochettes; a 200-strong record collection; and, of course, lots of delicious bread.

@hay_pan_ TEL +591 77257455

24 CORDIAL

Av. Almte. Miguel Grau 810, Barranco 15063, Peru

TO VISIT
BEFORE YOU DIE
BECAUSE

It hits all the right notes with some great dishes and a fine selection of locally produced natural wines

Opened in 2022, Cordial is located in Lima's Barranco, a bohemian district known for its street art and great restaurants. And it's the perfect fit for this hip bar that focuses on great food, great music and great natural wines. Featuring concrete and wood interiors with sunny yellow chairs, it was co-founded by Vanessa Touzard and Andrés Marroquín Winkelmann, who designed it as the perfect spot to house his exhaustive record collection. Originally, Cordial was meant to be mostly about music and coffee, in the style of Tokyo's audiophile cafés, but when the owners found this space with its large cellar, the project turned to celebrating natural wines. Working together with local experts at La Gastrónoma, they have created a menu presenting rare local wines by wineries such as Pepe Moquillaza, and produced their own wine: a Syrah-Malbec rosé and Italia-Torontel, made with the help of Ismael Carpio from Pampas de Ica. These can be paired with snacks such as *boquerones* and dishes that include a carrot salad named after Patti Smith, *porchetta tonkatsu* and a chocolate ganache with Peruvian coffee.

@cordial_barranco

TEL +51 957 801 199

25 BAR COVELL

4628 Hollywood Blvd, Los Angeles, CA 90027, USA

TO VISIT
BEFORE YOU DIE
BECAUSE

This script-worthy bar with no wine list keeps the conversation about wine flowing with brio

Located in LA's Los Feliz neighbourhood, Bar Covell is a fittingly cinematic kind of place, with an old-style cosy décor featuring vintage cameras, dim Edison bulbs and even the odd motorcycle on the wall. Founded by Matthew Kaner and Dustin Lancaster, the bar focuses on small production wines from all around the globe. All wines are available by the glass, and there is no written list. Instead, each guest is invited to tell the bartender what kind of wine they like or want. Tastes are poured, wines are discussed, and a favourite is chosen. The wine selection is constantly rotating, with the hope that guests will find new options every time they pull up a stool at the bar. These might include a French Domaine Leon Barral Faugères Grenache and Champagne Fleury Blanc de Noirs Brut, or a Californian Rock Wall Wine Company Tannat. There's also a great choice of beers, and a food menu that offers cheese plates, skewers of chorizo and dates, 'devilish' eggs and rosemary tater tots. And if you can't bear to leave, there is a beautifully appointed boutique hotel upstairs.

barcovell.com TEL +1 323 660 4400

26 ESTERS

1314 7th St, Santa Monica, CA 90401, USA

TO VISIT
BEFORE YOU DIE
BECAUSE

The perfect place for people watching and bottle sampling in the heart of downtown Santa Monica

Taking its name from the compounds that contribute to a wine's aroma, Esters is a stylish wine bar and shop located in Santa Monica's historic Telephone Building, a 1937 Art Deco landmark. It was recently selected as a semifinalist for the 2023 James Beard Outstanding Bar Award. 'My hope is that Esters is that kinda-cosy and kinda-fancy, but still chill place to hang out, where you can stay for 30 minutes or three hours,' says co-owner and wine director Kathryn Coker. Enjoy its expansive patio and browse its 250+ wine collection from small producers and boutique wineries with farming practices focused on soil health, including great Burgundy (Coker's favourites) and funky biodynamic wines. At least 30 wines are poured by the glass at any given time, and guests can explore new vintages to pair with cheese and charcuterie during Sunday wine tastings and Monday cellar nights. Signature dishes include chicken escabeche, a market platter of marinated vegetables served with housemade lavash, and Belgian waffles.

esterswineshop.com TEL +1 310 899 6900

FLEURETTE
CELLAR

HOUR!
WORLD
FRANCE
ITALY
USA
SPARKLING

27 BAR BANDINI

2150 Sunset Blvd, Los Angeles, CA 90026, USA

TO VISIT BEFORE YOU DIE BECAUSE

Located on Sunset Boulevard, LA's first natural wine bar definitely deserves a close-up

Located in LA's Echo Park, an area once at the epicentre of the early local film industry and now known as the city's hippest neighborhood, Bar Bandini is named after one of the characters of local writer John Fante. Founded in 2015 by a trio of friends, Michael Lippman, Joshua Weinstein and Jason Piggott, it's a dark and moody space with a long sleek slate bar and wood-clad walls. An early pioneer of natural wines, it offers Californian wines on tap, as well as a selection of very popular orange and chilled red wines. On the list are wines by producers such as Cantina Indigeno, a collective that specialises in bringing abandoned vineyards back to life in Italy's Abruzzo region; and La Boutanche, a blend of Gamay from Anjou vinified by Frantz Saumon in his cellar in Montlouis. Foodwise, there are plenty of delicious snacks, as well as pop-ups by the likes of B'ivrit (Israeli-style vegan food) and One Hot Minute (plant-based Peruvian/Chinese cuisine). Also on the menu: a free comedy show every Wednesday night, featuring LA's vibrant comedic talent.

barbandini.com

28 WINE BAR BY CONCOURS MONDIAL DE BRUXELLES

Copenhague 23, Juárez, Cuauhtémoc, Mexico City, Mexico

TO VISIT BEFORE YOU DIE BECAUSE

You'll be spoiled for choice at the largest wine bar in Latin America, which only stocks award-winning bottles

Self-described as 'the UN of Fine Wines', the Concours Mondial de Bruxelles is an annual wine competition judged by a panel of 350 international experts that has become a reference in the industry. Although the organisation is based in Belgium, it chose Mexico City as the location for its first wine bar. Housed over three floors near the capital's Reforma Avenue, the bar stocks every wine with a medal from the competition (and on its top floor is the HQ of the Mexican sommelier school). Its wine library, the biggest in Mexico, holds over 3,000 labels from over 50 countries, ready to drink by the glass, bottle or tasting. Wines by the glass come in three different sizes (from 50 to 150 ml) and the selection changes every week. The gastronomic offering is designed to complement the wines rather than the other way round. Where else can you sample top bottles from Japan, Portugal and Mexico in one sitting?

winebarbycmb.com TEL +52 55 2211 0826

CONCOURS MONDIAL
BRUXELLES

29 LOCAL 1

Av. Álvaro Obregón 228, Roma Norte, Cuauhtémoc, Mexico City, Mexico

TO VISIT BEFORE YOU DIE BECAUSE

This pared-back, gallery-like wine bar is the ideal place to sample Mexican natural wines

Serving only natural wines, this industrial, minimalist space in Mexico City's Roma district comes with its own contemporary art gallery at the back and artist residency upstairs. It does serve a couple of platters–Mexican organic cheese and charcuterie, tinned fish, and a selection of In Situ mescals–but it's really all about the wine here. There's plenty available by the glass, for example a Cantina Indigneo from Abruzzo and a Milan Nestarec from the Czech Republic, as well as bottles produced closer to home, such as the Cava Garambullo Chardonnay from San Miguel Allende and Dominio de las Abejas Nebbiolo from Ojos Negros. The wine list includes Mexican options such as Bichi Pet Mex, a sparkling wine from a 69-year-old vineyard in Baja California, and an Octagono Vino Naranja with tropical notes of guava and pineapple. The friendly, knowledgeable team will help you discover a myriad of unusual wines. The extensive orange wine section comprises over 20 options from countries around the world.

local1.mx

TEL +52 55 5941 5257

30 VIGNERON

Jalapa 181, Roma Norte CP 06700, Mexico City, Mexico

TO VISIT
BEFORE YOU DIE
BECAUSE

It's a chic spot to enjoy a glass of champagne and take in Mexico City's buzzing Roma Norte district

Opened in December 2020, Vigneron is both a wine shop and wine bar that stands out from the crowd thanks to its funky décor of busy wallpaper, velvet upholstery and dark wood panelling. It specialises in small producers from Spain's Madrid, Terra Alta and Conca de Barbera regions and from all over France, from Val de Loire to Alsace. Vigneron is famous for its extensive champagne selection, which includes labels such as Huré Frères, Jacques Lassaigne, Le Brun Servenay and Marie Courtin. Another firm favourite is Burgundy, with wines by producers such as Sylvain Pataille, Jean-Noël Gagnard and François Mikulski. Its owners found inspiration in the French concept of 'cave à manger', so you can pair your wine with a dinner of soft-boiled egg toast with caviar and braised brisket with peppercorn sauce with triple-cooked French fries, followed by a *baba au rhum*. The talented team changes the by-the-glass selection daily, choosing great bottles such as a Charnay Beaujolais 2021 or Château Le Puy Emilien 2019 Merlot.

vigneron.mx

TEL +52 55 3543 3056

31 THE WINE BAR BY GRAND CRU

Metropolitan Center, Av. Lázaro Cárdenas 2400-Interior A2, Valle Oriente 66269, Mexico

TO VISIT BEFORE YOU DIE BECAUSE

You'll find excellent food and music at this chic wine bar, not to mention a great selection of Old World and Mexican wines

Grand Cru is Monterrey's leading fine-dining restaurant, so you can expect the same high-quality service and ingredients at this wine-focused offshoot. Located in Monterrey's fancy Metropolitan Center mall, it offers a great selection of French, Italian and Spanish wines, with a penchant for natural, non-intervention and biodynamic producers. 'We always try to showcase the work of small producers, deeply rooted in their terroir,' explains owner and sommelier Ludovic Anacleto, while his team are all trained sommeliers, including the hostess. Best-selling wines include Morgan from Domaine Lapierre; Loteria Sangiovese from Vinos Loteria in Mexico, a small, organic vineyard in San Miguel de Allende; Bodegas Chacra Barda and Querciabella Mongrana. All these can be paired with a selection of tapas made with local ingredients from Nuevo Leon, Coahuila and Guanajuato. Add to this a great neo-bistro décor featuring three chandeliers, each made out of 335 Riedel glasses, and some live music ranging from jazz to freestyle electro. All in all, you pretty much have the perfect setting to enjoy Mexico's best bottles.

@thewinebarmty

TEL +52 81 1359 9358

32 VINVINVIN

1290 rue Beaubien E, Montréal, QC H2S 1P9, Canada

TO VISIT
BEFORE YOU DIE
BECAUSE

Top quality wines and produce, in a friendly bar on a trendy street just a few steps away from the vast Jean-Talon Market

The first thing you notice at vinvinvin is the bright interiors and excellent branding–an illustration of a smiling face with three little Vs (by the happily named Catherine Potvin), is printed on the bar's wine glasses. It perfectly reflects the ethos of the place, 'designed in the spirit of the wines we like to drink–colourful, elegant, joyful, and with a lot of personality,' explains sommelier Nikolas Da Fonseca. The bar serves exclusively all-natural and organic wines, with a strong focus on Central European producers (mainly from Germany, Czechia, Austria and Hungary) as well as North American winemakers (especially those from north-eastern Quebec). The list changes weekly, so there's always something new to discover here. Foodwise, the menu is seasonal, but staples include homemade sourdough bread with brown butter and honey, and a baloney sandwich (the sausage is made using organic beef by a butcher friend). Vinvinvin prides itself on its friendly welcome and its ability to connect people, including top winemakers, farmers and fishermen.

vinvinvin.ca TEL

33 BOUNTY HUNTER

975 First Street, Napa, CA 94559, USA

TO VISIT BEFORE YOU DIE BECAUSE

This great wine bar, smokin' BBQ and bottle shop is the perfect pitstop while exploring California's Napa Valley wine region

Located in the heart of downtown Napa, Bounty Hunter offers the full Americana experience, from the bright neon signs at the front, to the saddle seats, hunting trophies, BBQ dishes and top selection of whiskeys inside. Obviously, given its location, it specializes in top wines from Napa and California, including Rombauer Chardonnay and Chateau Montelena Cabernet Sauvignon, although it also has fine bottles from Bordeaux, Tuscany and Champagne on the menu. You'll be truly spoiled for choice as the 18-page wine list features a line-up of over 400 wines, plus 40 wines available by the glass. These include a great choice of Californian wines, from sparkling wines such as Schramsberg's Mirabelle Brut, Sauvignon Blancs and Chardonnays from the likes of Liquid Farm, Merry Edwards and Cade, as well as Grgich Hills rosé, Bacigalupi Pinot Noir and Orin Swift Cabernet Sauvignon. Be sure to sample the food: Bounty Hunter is known for its Smokin' Barbeque Platter and Cajun-spiced Beer Can Chicken (served perched on a Tecate beer can).

bountyhunterwinebar.com TEL +1 707 226 3976

34 ALDO SOHM WINE BAR

151 W 51st St, New York, NY 10019, USA

TO VISIT BEFORE YOU DIE BECAUSE

This dynamic NYC destination by top sommelier Aldo Sohm has something for everyone

Just steps away from one of the world's top restaurants, Le Bernardin, is this wonderful casual-chic bar by celebrity sommelier Aldo Sohm (who is also Le Bernardin's wine director, Best Sommelier in the World 2008 and the author of the best-selling 2019 *Wine Simple* guide). The wine bar's extensive wine list, featuring regions in France, Italy, Germany and Aldo's home country of Austria and more, rotates regularly, offering guests over 40 options by the glass, 200 by the bottle, as well as a monthly flight programme and nightly 9pm pours from magnums. Here you can taste a wine from Tenerife (Suertes del Marqués Trenzado), Portugal (Hugo Mendes Lisboa Branco) and Greece (Assyrtiko, Koutsogiannopoulos, Santorini), or splash out on a magnum of Pierre Péters Blanc de Blancs. The food menu includes French classics such as charcuterie and *croque-monsieur*, while in winter, there's also fondue and mulled wine, made with Merlot and port wine simmered in a mixture of spices and orange peel.

aldosohmwinebar.com

TEL +1 212 554 1143

35 PARCELLE

135 Division St, New York, NY 10002, USA

TO VISIT
BEFORE YOU DIE
BECAUSE

Pair Asian-inspired bar snacks with Italian and French wines in this beautifully designed bar in Manhattan's Chinatown

Aiming to offer 'smart, delicious wines for every scenario in your life', Parcelle is an online wine store founded by Grant Reynolds and Josh Abramson. Painted in a pleasing vine-leaf green, its brick-and-mortar outpost in Chinatown features chic interiors by designer Paul Renwick, inspired by the French and Italian labels on the bar's wine list. Parcelle's inventory includes 2,982 bottles, all of which are available to purchase here without markup (the online wine list is very easy to navigate by grape, region or price). Behind the bar you will find expert sommeliers who will be able to recommend rarer wines, as well as an excellent food menu, with the chicken katsu sandwich a particular favourite. The by-the-glass selection includes daily changing orange, rosé and chilled red wines, as well as wines by producers such as Silvia Zucchi, Rafael Palacios and Nino Negri. There's also a great section of 'Bottles we think you should drink tonight', featuring the likes of a Savart champagne, Bernard Moreau Bourgogne Blanc and I Suoli Etna Rosso.

parcellewine.com TEL +1 212 258 0722

36 AIR'S CHAMPAGNE PARLOR

127 MacDougal St, New York, NY 10012, USA

TO VISIT
BEFORE YOU DIE
BECAUSE

You will find a great selection of bubblies from both historic producers and newcomers, in a classy, intimate setting

Accessed through the equally tempting Tokyo Record Bar is this champagne bar, decked out with unique pieces of furniture in a glamorous, NYC Art Deco style. Its owner, Ariel Arce, formerly of Riddling Widow and Birds & Bubbles, is a proponent of a more relaxed and accessible approach to a champagne bar that demystifies the sparkling wine. On the menu are bottles (many at accessible prices) by the likes of Pierre Gerbais, Christophe Mignon, R. Pouillon and Larmandier-Bernier, as well as treats such as oysters, Kaluga caviar sandwiches with brioche and egg yolk custard. The best-selling fries, perfectly crispy and served with a yuzu and truffle aioli, are a particularly good match for bubbly. (Chef Zach of Tokyo Record Bar also offers extra dishes to sample, usually seafood and dessert.) Among the team's latest favourites are Philipponnat, a champagne house founded in 1522; rising star Élise Bougy; and Frédéric Savart, whose L'Accomplie Premier Cru is said to be reminiscent of wildflower honey on toast.

airschampagneparlor.com TEL +1 212 420 4777

37 CORKBUZZ

13 E 13th St, New York, NY 10003, USA

TO VISIT BEFORE YOU DIE BECAUSE

There are wines from around the world, selected by award-winning sommeliers and served with market-fresh food in the Big Apple

Corkbuzz's Union Square flagship has year-round access to Union Square's greenmarket, which means it offers an ever-evolving Mediterranean menu – roasted pepper with chickpea panisse, *cavatelli cacio e pepe* – to pair with its selection of wines from all over the world. Founded by master sommelier Laura Maniec, Corkbuzz focuses on offering both an approachable yet varied selection of wines from the classical to the esoteric, and a series of masterclasses and events to share the extensive knowledge of beverage director Ryan Totman and his team. With a choice of over 30 wines, the by-the-glass selection includes the likes of a Fio Piu Piu *pét nat* from the Mosel and Zaro Pivol Malvazija from Slovenia, as well as big names such as Envínate and Château d'Yquem. Also on offer are the wine flights, which include a Sommelier Mixtape ('Put yourself in our hands with a few selections our sommeliers are excited about') and Drink Local, with a selection of New York wines from The Hamptons, Long Island and Finger Lakes. There is also another branch in Chelsea Market.

corkbuzz.com TEL +1 646 873 6071

38 THE PUNCHDOWN

1737 Broadway, Oakland, CA 94612, USA

TO VISIT BEFORE YOU DIE BECAUSE

This award-winning natural wine specialist organises winemaker tastings, food pop-ups and a monthly natural wine club

Having met while working harvest jobs in Sonoma Wine Country, owners D.C. Looney and Lisa Costa realised they shared a passion for natural wines, and went on to open The Punchdown in Oakland in 2009. It was an excellent move: the pair was selected a semifinalist for the prestigious James Beard Award for Outstanding Wine Program–the only business selected in all of California. This nomination is partly based on their clear vision of natural wines: many of the bottles the Punchdown stocks are 'zero-zero', the most extreme form of natural winemaking in which nothing at all is added or removed, and they prefer wines that are hand-harvested, hand-sorted and produced on 'more than organic' vineyards. There are 25 wines by the glass every day (as well as special flights), by producers such as Lucy Margaux, Domaine Binner and Matassa, while bar snacks range from homemade soups and salads to Minerva Conservas. It's a recipe for success, and the duo is due to open another bar in nearby Sebastopol.

punchdownwine.com TEL +1 510-788-7877

39 LE CAVEAU BAR

614 S. 7th St, Philadelphia, PA 19147, USA

TO VISIT
BEFORE YOU DIE
BECAUSE

This slice of France in the heart of Philly offers an award-winning selection of French wines and comprehensive tasting sessions

Located above The Good King Tavern in Philly's Bella Vista, Le Caveau is a Parisian-inspired joint with French disco blasting from the speakers and plates of *saucisson*, *tapenade* and *fromage* on the tables. Its exhaustive wine list, curated by owner and wine director Chloé Grigri, is naturally French-focused, with over 130 bottles and an assortment of wines by the glass, many sustainably farmed or natural wines. Among Grigri's favourite producers are artisan champagne maker Christophe Mignon; Alice Bouvot, a natural wine producer from Jura; Les Sablonnettes in the Loire Valley; and the Austrian Jutta Kalchbrenner, who makes traditionally inspired wines from old vine parcels in the middle of Vienna. Opened in late 2019, Le Caveau wasted no time to impress, becoming a James Beard Award semi-finalist for Outstanding Wine Program in 2020, and Outstanding Bar in 2023. Come for the monthly themed Night Class and Study Group sommelier-led tastings, and stay for a delicious homemade *mousse au chocolat*.

lecaveaubar.com TEL +1 510 788 7877

40 BAR MARCO

2216 Penn Ave, Pittsburgh, PA 15222, USA

TO VISIT
BEFORE YOU DIE
BECAUSE

This small but mighty wine bar and restaurant offers an award-winning experience in Pittsburgh's Strip District

Founded in 2011 by a trio of childhood friends, Bar Marco is located in a former redbrick firehouse, and initially became known for its great cocktails and Italian fare (arancini, gnocchi, orecchiette and Piedmontese specialties). More than a decade later, it is also much appreciated for its excellent wine programme, which has helped diners discover natural wines and varietals from lesser-known Italian provinces. Whether you're sitting at the busy bar, or in the wine room in the whitewashed cellar, you can taste natural/low-intervention wines from small-scale producers such as a Rosso Piceno from Italy's Azienda Santa Barbara and Muscadet Sèvre et Maine by France's Château de la Gravelle. Every night there are about six to eight different wines by the glass in addition to the bottle list. Unusual for the USA, the bar doesn't operate on a tip model; its expert, longstanding staff members are paid a living wage with benefits and health insurance, and go on research trips together to Piedmont.

barmarcopgh.com TEL +1 412-471-1900

41 STEM WINE BAR

3920 N Mississippi Avenue, Portland, OR 97227, USA

TO VISIT BEFORE YOU DIE BECAUSE

This gem of a small business is a great place to discover both French and Oregonian lesser-known wines

After a rocky start–it opened just before the pandemic lockdowns and had to instantly pivot into virtual wine tastings–this small wine bar is fast becoming a local favourite. It's the passion project of Wei-En Tan, a Singaporean native who spent many years of her youth working with her family in vineyards in Bordeaux and Burgundy. A trained pilot and a graduate of three of the top US universities, Wei-En eventually moved to Portland and fell in love with Oregonian wines. Apparently, the climate of Willamette Valley in Oregon is extremely similar to that of Burgundy in France. Local favourites include Elk Cove and Firesteed wines. Wei-En says her goal at Stem is 'to create an "Oregon Meets the World" menu focused on flights and glass options, with no judgment or pretension, so everyone can taste as many wines as they can, or revisit old favourites in good company.' There are over 150 wines on the menu, including plenty of natural, biodynamic and organic bottles.

stemwinebarpdx.com TEL +1 503 477 7164

42 THE WINEHOUSE

Rua Paulo Barreto 25, Rio de Janeiro, RJ 22280-010, Brazil

TO VISIT BEFORE YOU DIE BECAUSE

In a country where cold beer is the drink of choice, this is a true haven for wine lovers and the place to discover Brazilian wines

For years, the only place to drink wine in Rio was in expensive restaurants and hotel lobbies. Which is why fellow wine enthusiasts Dominic Parry, a Brit, and his wife Selene, a Brazilian, decided to open WineHouse in 2014. The small bar was packed from the start, and with good reason: it was the perfect spot to discover locally made wine, as many Brazilian themselves weren't familiar with their country's fine wines (although there are also wines from abroad, including Argentina and France). Dominic 'wholeheartedly recommends trying a natural Brazilian wine, such as Vin de Soif, a 100 per cent Gamay from the South of Brazil which sits between the rosé and red category.' Although they have an increasing number of natural wines on their menu, the pair aim to stay democratic and have a varied selection of bottles from smaller wineries. Wines by the glass include Brazilian rosé from Bodega Sossego and sparkling wine from Pedres Brut, while bar snacks include locally made cheese and charcuterie, and delicious variations on the humble bruschetta.

@winehouse_rio

TEL +55 21 99209 1773

43 BIRBA

458 Grove St, San Francisco, CA 94102, USA

TO VISIT BEFORE YOU DIE BECAUSE

A quiet oasis away from the chaos of the city, with a comprehensive selection of wines from all corners of the globe

Located in San Francisco's Hayes Valley, this cosy wine bar, housed in a former filling station, comes with a great patio and street-side parklet on which to enjoy the best wines from around the world. Its well-travelled owner, sommelier Angela Valgiusti, earned the nickname Birba or 'little troublemaker', while living in Italy. It was the perfect name for her dream project, this 'magic little spot', which aims to recreate the feel of the cute cafés she discovered while travelling in Spain. There are small plates of antipasti, plus by-the-glass wines including the likes of Ameztoi Hijo de Rubentis from the Basque Country; natural wine by Hungary's Domaine Bükk; and Californian Folk Machine Charbono from the nearby Suisun Valley. The by-the-bottle menu, with wines from Slovenia, Sardinia and Sonoma, is peppered with recommendations (Zidarich 2019 'is one of our favourite skin-contact wines') and there's even Eins Zwei Zero Alcohol-Free Riesling from Germany's Leitz.

birbawine.com TEL +1 415 549 7612

44 BUDDY

3115 22nd St, San Francisco, CA 94110, USA

TO VISIT
BEFORE YOU DIE
BECAUSE

Located in San Francisco's Mission District, Buddy is a friendly neighbourhood bar with top-notch food and wine

Featuring long tan leather banquettes, checkerboard flooring and a cute record player on a vintage cabinet, this cosy wine bar is the result of great teamwork by a bunch of friends. Sharing decades of combined experience in the industry, they first launched a Kickstarter campaign to make their dream a reality. Buddy opened its doors in 2021 and has been going from strength to strength since, thanks, of course, to its great wine selection, which includes a Baccabianca by Tenuta Grillo; a white wine for lovers of skin contact; Californian wines such as Iruai Winery's Lounge Lizard Rosé, which is 'wild, rocky and with big blackberry energy'; and De Levende Fred's Roby Red, 'a juicy, ripe old-school farmer's blend' from the Redwood Valley. On Sean Thomas's food menu are perfectly presented small plates, dips and crudités, including irresistible *gougères* with smoked trout roe and bay leaf labneh, as well as Chinese, Hawaiian, Venezuelan and Baja-style Mexican dishes by a talented roster of pop-up chefs.

buddythebar.com

45 BARRICA 94

Av. José Alcalde Délano 10533, Local 1508, Lo Barnechea, Región Metropolitana, Chile

TO VISIT BEFORE YOU DIE BECAUSE

A busy bar with a friendly team, this is a great place to sample the best of Chilean food and wine

Located in a high-end open-air shopping mall in Santiago's Los Trapenses neighbourhood, Barrica 94 has become a hub for oenophiles. The bright and welcoming space offers around 15 different wines by the glass and a 250-bottle-strong wine list. Among them are the likes of Pinot Gris Aconcagua de Errazuriz Single Vineyard 2016; Cabernet Sauvignon de Bodega Re Cabergnan 2011; and a wide range of local winemakers, from the small scale (Viña Maturana, Casa Marin) to the bigger names (Odfjell, De Martino). The Chilean wines are paired with local dishes, from machas clams baked with Parmesan and *chorrillana* (French fries topped with sliced meats and fried eggs) to chocolaty *cuchufli* biscuits. The best way to sample all this is to try a wine flight, such as 'Chile is not just about red wines', or themed flights that highlight the terroirs of the cooler coastal regions such as the Casablanca Valley. Owners Alberto Bitrán and Karen Milgram and their team always extend a warm welcome— and it's open on Sundays too.

barrica94.cl

TEL +56 2 3210 2200

46 BOCANÁRIZ

José Victorino Lastarria 276, Santiago, Region Metropolitana, Chile

TO VISIT BEFORE YOU DIE BECAUSE

There's no better place for a crash course in the wealth and breadth of the Chilean winemaking world

In just over a decade, this wine bar in the historical neighbourhood of Barrio Lastarria has become a must-visit for wine lovers looking to learn all about local wines. Bocanáriz's team of bilingual sommeliers guide visitors through the wide variety of grapes and origins, with the help of an all-Chilean wine list that includes over 250 labels, from the cutting-edge Tabalí and De Martino to the pioneering Miguel Torres and Javiera Ortúzar. Featuring wines such as Ventisquero Sauvignon Blanc from Atacama and Santa Rita Bougainville Petite Syrah from Maipo Valley, the wine by-the-glass selection comes in two sizes (50cc and 150cc), with bottles preserved using the Enomatic system. The Bocanáriz Flights menu offers 12 different thematic tastings of three glasses each. The wine bottles are perfectly kept in Bocanáriz's 20m² cellar. Originally built in the early 1920s, the bar holds 2,400 bottles and is the perfect spot to host small tasting sessions and enjoy a cold platter or ceviche.

bocanariz.cl TEL +56 2 2638 9893

47 ENOTECA SAINT VINSAINT

Rua Professor Atilio Innocenti, 811, Vila Nova Conceição, São Paulo, Brazil

TO VISIT BEFORE YOU DIE BECAUSE

Celebrating all things local, fresh and seasonal, this charming *enoteca* offers all the classics, plus homemade liquors and infusions

A pioneer in the movement of natural, organic and biodynamic wines in Brazil, Enoteca Saint VinSaint was founded by Lis Cereja in 2008. Not only is it an excellent wine bar, with a lovely bohemian atmosphere, it's also a great champion of local and circular economy, working with 100 per cent organic producers around the State of São Paulo. It even has its own organic gardens, where the team grows the herbs and spices for its mostly plant-based food menu, and which are key to creating the homemade liquors, teas and infusions, as well as *jaboticaba* wines, one of the house's specialties. There are around 400 labels each month, which are rotated by the glass or bottle. Priority is given to Brazilian wines such as Era dos Ventos, Bella Quinta and Faccin, but there are plenty of European and American wines both on the menu and in the bottle shop.

saintvinsaint.com.br TEL +55 11 3846 0384

48 VALLEY

487 1st West, Sonoma, California, CA 95476, USA

TO VISIT
BEFORE YOU DIE
BECAUSE

This family run business in bustling Sonoma offers Californian dreaming in spades

This neighbourhood wine bar and restaurant is located on Sonoma Plaza in an old adobe building built in 1838. 'Our mission at Valley is to provide simple, delicious food matched with domestic and imported wines that we feel passionate about,' say the owners, who favour producers using biodynamic, permaculture, ancestral methods and regenerative agriculture in the vineyards, 'with little to no messing around in the winery'. Run by two couples, Emma and Steph (in the kitchen) and Lauren and Tanner (front of house), Valley makes its own table wine and organises wine tastings by labels including Dunites Wine Co. and Grape Ink. Its California home cooking is also worth a mention. Influenced by the myriad cultures that make California interesting, it includes dishes such as Crispy Rice, made with locally grown short-grain rice, house olive oil cake and XO egg, a simple boiled egg from a local farm with house-made XO sauce.

valleybarandbottle.com

TEL +56 2 2638 9893

49 BAR GOBO

237 Union St, Vancouver, BC V6A 2B2, Canada

TO VISIT BEFORE YOU DIE BECAUSE

This dynamic space is in constant evolution, so who knows what you'll discover on your next visit

Bar Gobo dubs itself 'the wine bar at the end of the world', even though it's located in bustling downtown Vancouver. A visit here is a real journey: the bar was conceived as a progressive platform showcasing the work of up-and-coming chefs and sommeliers. The current residents are chef Jiwon Seo, who brings her unique twist on local, seasonal food with a Korean accent (produced from a tiny corner kitchen, her creations include caramelised leek waffle and persimmon cake); and sommelier Peter Van de Reep, who was crowned the 2020 British Columbia Sommelier of the Year. The wine programme, with a preference for organic and biodynamic producers, includes Canadian labels such as Therianthropy and Tantalus. The rotating selection of around 30 wines by the glass 'that surprise and intrigue' reflects Van de Reep's enthusiasm and deep knowledge. Among his current favourites are Cappellano Barolo Chinato, Collestefano Verdicchio di Matelica and JJ Prum Wehlener Sonnenuhr Riesling Kabinett.

bargobo.com

TEL +1 604 423 5400

50 FLIGHT WINE BAR

777 6th St NW, Washington, DC 20001, USA

TO VISIT BEFORE YOU DIE BECAUSE

This award-winning bar has it all, from an inspiring wine programme and great ambiance to wine flights for all tastes

Flight Wine Bar in Washington's Chinatown was founded in 2014 by Kabir Amir and Swati Bose, who both ditched their former careers in finance and law to retrain as sommeliers. It was a great decision, especially since their bar was nominated a James Beard Semifinalist for Outstanding Wine Program in 2020 and 2023. The pair travelled the world to select the labels for their award-winning wine list, which focuses on small, family-owned estates and features 750 wines, including over 35 wines by the glass. Also available are 22 different wine flights, all with great names, such as 'Nothing Wrong With a Little Skin Contact', which features Czech, Slovenian and Georgian winemakers; while The Acid Trip showcases wines by Austria's Schloss Gobelsburg, Portugal's Anselmo Mendes, and Sicily's Tenuta Tascante. On the dinner menu are small plates of garlic butter shrimps and Japanese eggplants.

flightdc.com TEL +1 202-864-6445

51 SHIRAZ

Lijnbaansgracht 267 HS, 1017 RL, Amsterdam, Netherlands

TO VISIT BEFORE YOU DIE BECAUSE

This atmospheric bar in the historic centre of Amsterdam has been voted the best wine bar in the Netherlands

A stone's throw away from the Rijksmuseum lies another treasure trove, Shiraz, dedicated not to art but to wine, and more precisely to the dark-skinned grape variety of Syrah, also known as Shiraz. 'Like the Shiraz grape, the atmosphere is a blend of Middle Eastern and traditional French in a contemporary translation,' say the canal-side bar owners, Anita Boezaard and Wim Wiersma. There are more than 260 wines on the menu, all clearly labelled with adjectives such as spicy, heavy or mineral. But if you are dazzled by so much choice, you can chat with the sommelier for advice. There are around 30 by-the-glass wines by producers such as Domaine Tempier (France), Rapariga da Quinta (Portugal) and Château Purcari (Moldova), and you can taste a couple of bottles by Dutch producer Wijngoed Thorn. Snackwise, there's everything from oysters to cheese croquettes and vegan empanadas. And if you like the wine you tasted, you can stock up at the adjoining boutique.

 shirazamsterdam.nl

52 BUBBLES & WINES

Nes 37, 1012 KC, Amsterdam, Netherlands

TO VISIT BEFORE YOU DIE BECAUSE

A welcome and elegant oasis for wine and champagne lovers in the bustling heart of Amsterdam

Avoid the touristy Dam Square and head straight to Bubble & Wines, which opened in 2005 on a small lane in central Amsterdam with the aim of pouring high-quality wines by the glass. There's currently a choice of about 45 labels, all available by bottle, glass or tasting (half-glass), and all selected by Sven and Johnny, the two wine enthusiasts who run Bubbles & Wines. 'You don't have to be a wine connoisseur to come to our bar,' they say. 'Tell us what you like and we'll tell you which wines you should try.' On the perfectly curated wine programme is a light and floral Apostelhoeve white wine from Maastricht; a light red from Wairau River in New Zealand; and a rosé from Domaine Le Pive in Camargue. Also available by the glass are sweet wines, port and sherry. The High Wines experiences offers the chance to sample both wines and nibbles: for example, a *spumante* is paired with a grilled cheese sandwich with truffle, while a Bergère Champagne Blanc de Blancs is served with caviar, blinis and crème fraîche.

bubblesandwines.com TEL +1 202 864 6445

53 TA-NNIN

Volkstraat 50, 2000 Antwerp, Belgium

TO VISIT BEFORE YOU DIE BECAUSE

This funky urban wine bar is a welcoming place offering a variety of wines by the glass

Love brought Tawat Hattatammanoon all the way from Thailand to Belgium, where he ended up working in a restaurant and an Italian wine bar. 'I got the wine virus from my father-in-law,' he says. 'My dream was to open a wine bar myself.' Mission accomplished with Ta-nnin, which he opened in 2020 after completing his sommelier training. A wonderful little bar in Antwerp Zuid, near the fashion district of Sint-Andries, it is designed as 'an easygoing, urban wine bar where everybody feels welcome'. The funky décor includes green walls, cosy lighting and leather straps used as bottle holders, while the wine list offers over 170 different wines from all over the world, focused on indigenous grape varieties from the regions they come from. There's a diverse, frequently updated by-the-glass list comprising labels such as Spain's El Hato y el Garabato, South Africa's Oldenburg, and Belgium's very own Haksberg. The most popular small plates on the seasonal menu are the Korean beef gyoza and the hummus Tandoori.

tannin.be

TEL +32 470 10 44 83

U RIJOT

54 CAVA VEGERA

Posidonos 11, Voula 166 73, Greece

TO VISIT
BEFORE YOU DIE
BECAUSE

Sip on the best wines and enjoy a slice of Greek hospitality on a bustling terrace in Athens' seaside district of Voula

Established in 1998, Cava Vegera started out as a shop selling wine and other delicacies, including chocolates and whiskies from producers all over Europe. In 2015, it opened its own bar, the first 'hybrid' bottle shop and bar in Greece. 'We believe that wine—whether you're buying it or selling it, and especially when you're drinking it —should be full of fun,' says founder Niotakis Konstantinos. 'What gets us really excited is when guests taste our special wines, which are difficult to find, but we've got hundreds of them.' The enthusiastic team, which comprises six sommeliers and four oenologists, loves to share their knowledge with guests. Among their latest picks are a Decugnano dei Barbi red from Umbria, and Tenet Wines 'The Pundit' from Washington's Columbia Valley. Cava Vegera also has a great collection of luxury wines, with a vintage to suit every taste, from Napa Valley icons and Tuscan classics to Australian treats. And, of course, you can enjoy all of these with great food, from fresh brunches to homemade pasta dishes.

@cavavegera

TEL +30 21 1012 5700

55 HETEROCLITO

2 Fokionos & Petraki, Athens 105 63, Greece

TO VISIT BEFORE YOU DIE BECAUSE

Discover the little-known world of Greek wines in the shadow of Acropolis Hill with the help of the bar's experts

In the historic centre of Athens is this great wine bar founded in 2012 by wine lovers Madeleine Lorantos and Dimitris Koumanis, who wished to 'highlight, with simplicity, the native varieties of vine and the wealth of Greek land'. Unsurprisingly, given the pair's passion for oenology, and enthusiasm for sharing it, it was a swift success. Today here you will find over 200 Greek labels, with an emphasis on natural wines, and a monthly changing selection of wines by the glass. Cold snacks include a delicious Greek cheese platter, while among the most popular bottles are Tetramythos's Roditis Nature, a white from the northern Peloponnese; Stavropoulos Estate's Coralli rosé from the western Peloponnese; and Oenos Nature's Naousa, a red from Macedonia. The beautifully put-together menu with tasting notes and winery information, offers, among other treasure finds, bottles from the Vegoritis Winery in Amyndeon and the Karageorgos Organic Vineyards in central Greece. All labels can be purchased at cellar prices.

heteroclito.gr

TEL +30 21 0323 9406

56 OINOSCENT

45 Voulis St, Syntagma, Athens 10558, Greece

TO VISIT
BEFORE YOU DIE
BECAUSE

Over 1,000 bottles to choose from in an atmospheric bar run by the country's top sommelier

Athens' first contemporary wine bar, Oinoscent opened its doors in 2008 and soon became a meeting point for wine lovers. They came in such droves that the bar had to move to a bigger space across the street a few years later. Its wine list offers 60 different wines by the glass, but its strong point is the cellar, which ages more than 1,000 labels, combining Greek (Domaine Karanika, Thymiopoulos Vineyards, Akrathos Newlands Winery, Gaia Estate) and international grape varieties. All were selected by owners Danis Agapitos and Aris Sklavenitis (who has won the Best Greek Sommelier contest no fewer than three times) and their team of six sommeliers, who will guide you through the dizzying choice. In the kitchen, chef John Tsikoudakis offers a complete experience of food and wine pairing with dishes such as Waldorf tuna and carob brownie. Plus, there's a selection of Greek craft beers, cheese and charcuterie to taste.

oinoscent.gr

TEL +30 21 0322 9374

57 BAR BRUTAL

Carrer de la Princesa, 14, Barcelona 08003, Spain

TO VISIT
BEFORE YOU DIE
BECAUSE

They do things differently here, with a truly exciting selection of pioneering natural wines and great Catalan labels

Barcelona's Bar Brutal is known for its extensive natural wine menu, listing wines from Catalonia, Spain, France, Italy, Georgia, Germany, Slovenia and Austria, with, uniquely, cuvees as old as 10-12 years. Its international team (currently combining 13 different nationalities) selects the best of Catalan wine—including Còsmic and Amós Bañeres—and work with winemakers to have exclusive Brutal cuvees. International labels featured include Italy's Bodega Lammidia and France's Matassa. Half of the food menu is vegetarian and vegan, and star dishes include octopus, tuna Mojama, deconstructed lemon crumble and liquorice flan. Just as unusual are the interiors, designed by Stefano Colombo and featuring furniture by Ramon de los Heros and papier-mâché sculptures by Tom Campbell. They have also just opened El Corner, a private tasting room in an adjoining space, and organise pop-ups such as Japanese brunches and *tacos y chupe* nights.

barbrutal.com TEL +34 933 19 98 81

58 NOBLE ROT

Gärtnerstraße 6, 10245 Berlin-Friedrichshain, Germany

TO VISIT BEFORE YOU DIE BECAUSE

This cool Berlin bar specialising in Hungarian dessert wines is great for those with a sweet tooth

This small neighbourhood bar in Berlin's hip Friedrichshain neighbourhood specialises in German and Hungarian wines, with the majority being either natural or low-intervention wines. 'The wines come to us directly from the winemaker, which is why you always find some rarities on our menu that were produced in very small quantities,' explains co-founder Szabolcs Bakti, who has visited, together with the team, all the wineries they feature. These include an exciting selection of 25 open white, red and sweet wines, and bottled wine from the wine regions of Ahr, Mosel, Nahe, Franken, Pfalz, Württemberg, Baden, Eger, Tokaj and Villany. The bar also collaborates with the renowned patisserie Jubel in nearby Prenzlauer Berg, which provides the desserts to accompany the Hungarian sweet wines that are their specialty. The bar is named after the noble rot that is key to producing the world-famous Tokaji Aszú dessert wines, and here you can try around five dessert wines by the glass, including some from 1999.

weinbar-berlin.com

TEL +49 30 22600377

59 DR MAURY

Schönhauser Allee 62, 10437 Berlin-Prenzlauer Berg, Germany

TO VISIT BEFORE YOU DIE BECAUSE

This cool Prenzlauer-Berg hanghout doesn't take itself too seriously—but is dead set on offering the best wines and dishes

Opened in 2018, this Prenzlauer Berg wine bar focuses on organic and natural wines, most of which are directly imported from France, Italy and Spain. Born in Germany and raised in France, sommelier Alex Kastner honed his skills at Michelin-starred restaurants around the world before moving to Berlin and joining Dr Maury in 2021. Among his favourites on the wine list are Orange Pig and Saveur from Les Vins Pirouettes, a collective of Alsatian winegrowers committed to organic farming, and Bumblebee from Hungarian winemaker Hummel. And his enthusiasm is catching: he's recruited two former customers and fellow wine lovers, Jonathan and Leyla, to manage front of house, and enticed young French chef Max to stay in Berlin, where he now prepares dishes such as spicy Asian-style roast beef, *œuf cocotte* with truffle oil, and Jerusalem artichoke hummus. Recently the team began offering a monthly Sunday brunch, serving Japanese sake and the traditional shot of Papidoux Calvados.

@drmauryberlin

60 FREUNDSCHAFT

Mittelstraße 1, Mitte, 10117 Berlin, Germany

TO VISIT BEFORE YOU DIE BECAUSE

An ode to friendship and fun, this underground bar is a little slice of Austria in the middle of the German capital

Located in Berlin's student district, just a short walk from Unter den Linden and Museum Island, Freundschaft was opened in 2018 by two rising stars, Austrian sommeliers Willi Schlögl and Johannes Schellhorn. 'The focus on our wine programme is a producer-based, undogmatic (in terms of sulphites) and quality-driven list with over 650 handpicked labels,' they say. Step down into this basement bar to discover a 26-metre-long oval oak counter, where you can sit and taste a series of wines mostly from Austria (including Kirchmayr, Christoph Hoch and Alwin & Stefanie Jurtschitsch), Germany, Burgundy and northern Italy. The constantly changing by-the-glass selection includes 15 sparkling, white, rosé, red and sweet wines, and an additional 15 fortified wines, including Graham's port. Completing the offering are Austrian dishes such as Spinatknödel—spinach dumplings with brown butter and smocked cheese, and a cooked ham from the Thum butchery in Vienna.

istdeinbesterfreund.com TEL +49 30 80492444

61 ORA

Oranienplatz 14, 10999 Berlin, Germany

TO VISIT BEFORE YOU DIE BECAUSE

This stunning wine bar has a wine programme ranging from classic to funky

Located in a former pharmacy dating to the 1860s, this elegant bar is lined with original glass cabinets and deep green leather banquettes. After a rocky start (it opened during the COVID-19 pandemic) it is now thriving, with sommelier Amyna Le managing a list of over 200 wines. 'Some wines are very classic in style and some are wild and funky,' she explains, 'but we are very thoughtful about what we offer as we want our wines to reflect of what we are trying to achieve at Ora in terms of working with small-scale sustainable and ethical producers.' Wine by the glass ranges from a Jeaunaux-Robin champagne to a Valdespino sherry. Otherwise, there is an extensive bubbly section with around 20 labels and a great choice of bottles from all around the world, including Germany's Langen Erben, Wasenhaus and Geltz Zilliken wineries. They will be perfectly paired with chef Sam Kindillon's delicate modern European dishes.

ora.berlin TEL +49 30 50955889

RANIEN-APOTHEKE

Mosel-Riesling
Kabinett 2016
trocken
SYBILLE KUNT

62 KINK

Schönhauser Allee 176, 10119 Berlin, Germany

TO VISIT
BEFORE YOU DIE
BECAUSE

A hip restaurant and bar in one of Berlin's lesser-known districts that keeps its excellent wine list an open secret

Located in a former brewery, Kink is known for its innovative cocktails and spacious terrace. But there's also great wines to be found at this trendy bar and restaurant, with its impressive double-height ceiling and neon artwork by Swiss artist Kerim Seiler. British head sommelier Edric Kent has designed an impactful list of wines: 'The most important philosophy for our wine card is that a good wine is a good wine,' he says. 'Yes, we have a strong focus on low-intervention wines but this will not stop us from selecting wines made with a more interventional approach, if the end product expresses the grape, the terroir and the winemaker. We also want to celebrate the lost, forgotten and the underappreciated.' The idea here is to showcase wines following a feeling-driven approach rather than categorising by country or grape. Kent's favourites include a Steiermark Sauvignon Blanc from Austria, a Ignios Borja Perez from Tenerife and Domaine de Panisse Le Mazet from France's Rhône region.

kink-berlin.de

TEL +49 30 41207344

63 VINERIA FAVALLI

Via Santo Stefano 5a, 40125 Bologna, Italy

TO VISIT BEFORE YOU DIE BECAUSE

Favalli offers the quintessential Italian experience in Bologna: great wines, great food and a great setting

Vineria Favalli is located a few steps away from Bologna's Piazza Santo Stefano on a postcard-perfect street with medieval covered walkways. It started out in 2014 as a traditional wine shop, adding a fully fledged wine bar and restaurant next door a few years later. Besides its Italian home cooking—radicchio lasagna, *piadina* and *crescione* sandwiches and tortellini—it specialises in wines from the region, including Podere Il Saliceto's Bi Fri Frizzante and Il Farneto Giandòn Bianco. The walls are lined with bottles of local Pignoletto, Alionza, Trebbiano and Rosso Bologna wines, while a blackboard displays daily specials and details the by-the-glass offers. There's also a great selection of natural wines, unusual in this part of the world. The thing is, there's not much of a menu, so it's best to ask for advice and have a look around before making your choice. It's also worth checking out their event programme, as it includes special wine tastings by the likes of Chianti's Fattoria Pomona and Val delle Corti.

vineriafavalli.it TEL +39 051 295821

64 BAR À VIN

3 cours du 30 Juillet, 33000 Bordeaux, France

TO VISIT BEFORE YOU DIE BECAUSE

This is the place to try the full range of Bordeaux wines, served by enthusiastic young sommeliers in a magnificent building

One of Bordeaux's most famous sights is the giant place des Quinconces, and just around the corner, there's another address that is not to be missed: the Bar à Vin. Run by the city's wine council, the bar is located in a sumptuous 18th-century building with soaring ceilings and stained-glass windows. Even more impressive is the fact that it offers the entire Bordeaux range—reds, dry and sweet whites, rosés, clarets and sparkling wines—by the glass, at affordable prices and in high-quality glasses. Every wine is presented with an information sheet, and is served by young sommeliers, some of whom are undergoing training here. The monthly wine list features around 30 wines, such as Château Bonnet (Entre-Deux-Mers) and Château Coutet (Barsac), while the food menu zooms in on local ingredients, such as lamprey *à la bordelaise* (i.e. in red wine), and charcuterie platters including smoked duck-breast fillet and *gratton bordelais*. Happily, for non-drinkers, there is a great choice of mineral waters and grape juices from Bordeaux.

baravin.bordeaux.com TEL +33 5 56 00 43 47

R.BUTHAUD

65 BLEND

Kuipersstraat 6-8, 8000 Bruges, Belgium

TO VISIT
BEFORE YOU DIE
BECAUSE

This fun little wine bar offers a chilled space to discover great wines and munch on local croquettes

This wine bar and shop was founded nearly seven years ago by Luk De Rooze and Kees Dobbelaar, respectively awarded best sommelier of Belgium in 2002 and 2009. Both had previously worked in Michelin-starred restaurants such as Oud Sluis, and as wine importers for over 15 years. The next logical step was to open a wine bar in their hometown of Bruges, and we're very glad they did. Inspired by Italian-style wine bars, Blend boasts a large wall lined with a selection of more than 700 wines by the bottle – all can be enjoyed in the bar with a simple mark-up. The monthly changing by-the-glass selection comprises 30 wines, which are sourced mainly from Italy and South Africa, and a range of European countries, with a preference for labels helmed by female winemakers. As well as the usual cold platters, there is also a great selection of Belgian croquettes with 12 different flavours to pair with the various wines.

blendwijnhandel.be TEL +32 497 17 20 85

66 BAR DU CANAL

Rue Antoine Dansaert 208, 1000 Brussels, Belgium

TO VISIT BEFORE YOU DIE BECAUSE

This friendly neighbourhood joint specialises in natural wine and a selection of great plant-based dishes

Opened five years ago at the end of the stretch of fashionable boutiques on rue Antoine-Dansaert, this buzzing bar is named after the Canal de Bruxelles, a once neglected industrial area which is now enjoying a new lease on life. Now run by sommelier Léa Frémont Roussel, one of the original co-founders, the bar specialises in natural wines, and a food menu that avoids the usual cheese and cold meat platters to focus on vegetable-based dishes such as crispy potatoes with garlic and fresh herbs, homemade pasta or updates of the traditional mussels, here served with Nduja, peas and basil. On the wine list are Rieslings by the Alsatian Famille Hebinger, Splash sparkling *pét nat* made by Vincent Alexis of Château Barouillet in Bergerac, and Vieille Canaille Beaujolais by Domaine des Canailles. Add to this a chilled atmosphere, a great vintage bar and high ceilings, and you have a great little neighbourhood bar to while away your evenings.

@barducanal TEL +32 2 355 53 73

67 LE WINE BAR DES MAROLLES

Rue Haute 198, 1000 Brussels, Belgium

TO VISIT BEFORE YOU DIE BECAUSE

A unique wine bar was founded by an expert sommelier who also happens to be an antique and art lover

Set in a wine-coloured townhouse in Brussels' lively Sablon district, Le Wine Bar des Marolles is the passion project of Vincent Thomaes, a wine broker, art lover and antiquarian, who spent 26 years working with his brothers at the Michelin-starred restaurant Château du Mylord in Belgium's Hainaut province. Thomaes finally went solo in 2007, when he decided to open this charming bar and restaurant with a boutique section that sells no only wine but also works of art and antiques. The by-the-glass selection includes Syrah and Grenache blends from Mur-Mur-Lum in Provence, a Bianco d'Alessano orange wine from Puglia's Petracavallo; and a Marquise de Moulbaix Chardonnay from Belgium. There are both classic and natural wines, mostly from France's top producing regions (including the often-overlooked Jura and Savoie) as well a great choice of local gueuse beers. Chef Alex Van Kalck is at the helm of the restaurant, serving dishes such as steak tartare and cuttlefish tagliatelle.

lewinebardesmarolles.be TEL +32 2 503 62 50

68 POMPETTE

Møllegade 3, 2200 Copenhagen, Denmark

TO VISIT BEFORE YOU DIE BECAUSE

Named after the French word for tipsy, this fun little bar is the place to taste natural wine in Copenhagen

'Pompette specialises in natural wine, alive and wild, from winemakers that are conscious of their practices in the vineyards and in the cellar, who prioritise their relationship with the land, and who produce honest and expressive wines,' explains Dan Stewart, the manager of this great little bar in Copenhagen's Nørrebro neighbourhood. They work extensively with French and Austrian winemakers (but also with producers from other parts of Europe and the New World), with the aim of offering good wine without the usual high mark-ups. Customers enjoy wines by-the-glass on the terrace, with orange wines being the most popular throughout the year. There's also a 'chai', or wine room, which holds 200 constantly changing bottles and serves as a bottle shop and a space for customers to explore and get advice. Food includes lots of cheese and intriguing daily specials such as cold fried chicken, all made with local and seasonal ingredients.

@pompettecph

69 BAR'VIN

Skindergade 3, 1159 Copenhagen, Denmark

TO VISIT BEFORE YOU DIE BECAUSE

The attention to detail is key at this well-respected Danish wine bar, which stocks over 1,000 labels

Despite its name (which translates as 'just wine') Bar'Vin is about much more than wine. Located in the heart of Copenhagen, it's a beautifully laid-out space with lovely bentwood chairs and splashes of yellow on the wall. It's also a restaurant, serving dishes such as seasonal risotto and the Bar'Vin tartare, served with pickled brown beech, *piment d'Espelette*, capers and watercress. So, what about the wine? Well, there's plenty of choice here, both classic and natural, with over 1,000 labels and 70 wines served by the glass, all from European producers. These include a great selection of champagnes, as well as bottles by Danish organic natural winemaker Vexebo Vin. 'Other than quality we don't have many dogmas about wine, but we prefer clean juicy wines without too much extraction and barrel aging, especially in new casks,' explains founder Nils Thyge.

barvin.dk

TEL +45 33 12 58 03

NICOLAS

70 LOOSE CANON

29 Drury St, Dublin D02 RX95, Ireland

TO VISIT
BEFORE YOU DIE
BECAUSE

A perfect combination of three of the best things in life: wine, cheese and Irish hospitality

A cheese and wine shop by day and a cheese and wine bar by night, Loose Canon started with a bang in 2018, its smart concept an instant crowd-pleaser. Owners Kevin, a former cheesemaker, and Brian, a trained cabinetmaker who put his skills to good use in the space, have created an all-white yet welcoming place at the front of the 18th-century George's Street Arcade. The shop is stocked with 25 Irish cheeses and 120 wines, but we suggest you take a seat and sample one of their four cheese toasties. They are made with Irish meat and cheese (including a fantastic creamy blue made by Mike Thomson from Greater Belfast) and served with pickles and chutney. Kevin, who fell in love with natural wine while living in Paris, says: 'Some of our favourite wines are from the new generation of German winemakers: DB Schmitt, Andi Mann, Glow Glow. It's extraordinary to watch the scene there grow, and the beauty and diversity of these wines is stunning.'

loosecanon.ie

Loose

71 LE DI-VIN

9 Randolph Pl., Edinburgh EH3 7TE, UK

TO VISIT BEFORE YOU DIE BECAUSE

A French wine bar located in a former Polish church that offers the best bottles from around the world

Virginie Brouard arrived in Edinburgh in 1991 at the age of 19, with £90 in her pocket. After working in a top French restaurant and setting up her own place, La Petite Folie, in the heart of Edinburgh's West End, she jumped at the opportunity to take over the adjoining private chapel, built in the 1930s but left empty and in need of repair. The refurbished space, now with mezzanine seating, is the perfect backdrop for her award-wining wine bar, which offers over 100 wines by the bottle and over 30 by the glass. The food menu couldn't be more French (snails in garlic butter, raclette, goat's cheese tartine, a cheese platter with Chaource, Tomme and Reblochon, and crème brûlée) but the wines come from all over the world. The menu is full of great finds, such as Argentinian Ruca Malen Malbec, an organic Syrah from Domaine Aléofane Saint Joseph and Pommard by Christophe Vaudoisey from the Côte de Beaune.

ledivin.co.uk TEL 0131 538 1815

72 DIE WEINBANK WIRTSHAUS

Hauptstraße 44, 8461 Ehrenhausen, Austria

TO VISIT BEFORE YOU DIE BECAUSE

This award-winning inn, fine-dining restaurant and wine bar is an absolutely essential stop on the South Styrian Wine Road

Although it is little known in the rest of Europe, Die Weinbank is one of the brightest stars in Austria's wine world, and the beating heart of South Styria, the regional home to Südsteiermark wines. At the helm are chef Gerhard Fuchs, Gault & Millau Chef of the Year 2004, and sommelier Christian Zach, Gault & Millau Sommelier of the Year 2021. The inn boasts a catalogue of 4,200 labels, including one of the most comprehensive Austrian wine lists in the world. The inn serves about 30 wines by the glass, which you can enjoy on the summer terrace. Start with a 2021 Muskateller & Welschriesling, *pét nat*, and follow up with a 2015 Sauvage WG Oberer Guess Sauvignon Blanc by Christian Krampl. Be sure to tuck into Fuchs's beautifully presented take on traditional dishes, such as crispy pork roast with cabbage and dumplings. Recommended food and wine pairing include a char fillet with pumpkin, pickled wild mushrooms and spring herbs, enjoyed with a 2021 Sauvignon Blanc Vergiss Wein Nicht! by the Weingut Familie Temenvt in Berghausen.

dieweinbank.at TEL +43 3453 22291

ZUM
FUCHS
BAU

73 CHEZ BACCHUS

Cr de Rive 7, 1204 Geneva, Switzerland

TO VISIT BEFORE YOU DIE BECAUSE

A chic décor, a friendly team and a huge wine fridge full of great wines waiting to be tasted

Located in a 19th-century building, a few steps away from Geneva's gastronomic hub of La Halle de Rive, this wine hotspot originally opened as a shop in 1999. A bar and restaurant followed in 2019, serving great platters and French brasserie fare (from the ever-changing *plat du jour* for lunch, to classics such as *steak frites*). It's named after the Roman god of wine, which tells you all you need to know about the house's real specialty: the heavenly nectar produced by winemakers from Switzerland, France and beyond. The beautiful wine fridge is fully stocked (800 international references), and on display are a variety of wooden crates from big-name châteaux and smaller producers. On offer are around 40 wines by the glass, a selection accompanied by a friendly, personalised service no matter what your budget. If you have time to spend in the Lake Geneva area, Chez Bacchus has two other outposts in Gland and Gstaad – and make sure to visit the Lavaux vineyard terraces, a UNESCO World Heritage site stretching for about 30 km along the lake's northern shores.

caveaudebacchus.ch/fr/chez-bacchus TEL +41 22 312 41 72

74 BJÖRNS BAR

Viktoriagatan 12, 411 25 Gothenburg, Sweden

TO VISIT BEFORE YOU DIE BECAUSE

A Gothenburg institution that offers not only amazing wine, but also the finest bar food sourced from its fine-dining sister restaurant

A leading figure in Gothenburg's hospitality scene, Björn Persson is the man behind the Michelin-starred restaurant Koka. He describes this bar as 'the back pocket of Koka', which makes sense as it is tucked away under the fine-dining restaurant. He's keen to describe it as a totally un-snobbish place to sit back, relax and enjoy a glass of wine. The laid-back atmosphere is definitely a winner, and so is the food offering, which uses the same first-class ingredients as its upstairs neighbour and includes dishes such as ponzu ceviche and Mont d'or fondue (plus, the kitchen is open until 2am on weekends). 'We love wines from Europe,' says Björn. 'Our focus is on organic wines from small producers, but we also have a wide range of classic wines and serve older vintage by the glass using Coravin.' Here, you can sample a Cheverny Rouge by Luc Percher from the Loire, a Meursault by Frédéric Magnien in Bourgogne, or a Radikon by Slatnik in Italy's Venezia Giulia.

 bjornsbar.se TEL +46 31 701 79 79

75 MURU'S WINEBAR

Lönnrotinkatu 14, 00100 Helsinki, Finland

TO VISIT
BEFORE YOU DIE
BECAUSE

The wine-focused offshoot of one of the country's leading restaurants, this gem of a bar is worth a visit

Restaurant Muru in Helsinki is one the most acclaimed wine restaurants in Finland and has received several prizes and awards for its wine programme. So, it's no wonder they have opened their own winebar right around the corner from the original restaurant. It's a cosy place with checkerboard floor and sofas, and a daily changing selection of wines by the glass with a list with over 750 wines to choose from, from a Frank Phélan Saint-Estéphe 2016 to a Champagne Bollinger PN TX17. There's a different activity planned for each of the four evenings a week it's open: blind tastings on Wednesdays; champagne on Thursdays; the sommeliers open a special bottle from the cellar on Fridays; and thematic afternoon tastings on Saturdays. Not to be missed is Muru's famous weekly changing risotto, a selection of dishes including beef tartare, and snacks with fresh anchovies.

murudining.fi/en/winebar TEL +358 300 472339

76 APOTEK

Lapinlahdenkatu 1, 00180 Helsinki, Finland

TO VISIT BEFORE YOU DIE BECAUSE

One of Finland's top addresses, Apotek will boost your health with its historic interiors and great wine selection

Apotek opened in 2020 in a listed century-old pharmacy in central Helsinki. The setting is truly atmospheric: the pharmacy was still in use until the 2010s, and still has all of its original features intact, from the woodwork to the old medicine jars. Even the tables have history, as they used to sit in a very cute café in Lyon. It is owned by wine importers Carelia Wines, so its monthly changing menu reflects their portfolio, which includes beautiful wines such Ansgsar Clüsserath, Schloss Lieser, Arpepe, Philippe Pacalet and Overnoy. Head chef Ville Rainio works with a city farm to get the best of local produce, preparing dishes such as fish crudo and kohlrabi with herb polenta. 'We are known for our cheese plates,' explains manager Alice Järvinen. 'We usually have over eight different types which we usually try to pair with a beautiful Macvin du Jura. Our importing company really loves their French wines from the Jura and the Alps, so we have a solid selection on our wine list.'

viinibaariapotek.fi TEL +358 9 27090977

77 VIGNERON WINE HOUSE

Bereketzade, Felek Sk. No.2, 34421 Beyoğlu/İstanbul, Turkey

TO VISIT BEFORE YOU DIE BECAUSE

This beautiful cellar in Istanbul's old town is the ideal spot to discover Turkey's many wines

Hidden in plain sight in Istanbul's bustling Galata district is this stunning 150-year-old cellar, part of the DeCamondo Galata hotel. It is home to the Vigneron Wine House, where you can sample wines produced from all over Turkey and beyond. Discover wines from the Chamlija Winery, founded in 2000 in the Strandja Massif near Bulgaria; Anaxagoras, which produces great Chardonnays near the Aegean Sea; or Vinolus's Kalecik Karasi reds, from Central Anatolia. Choose from over 60 local red wines and just under 30 Turkish white wines, including six of each category available by the glass. Vigneron's knowledgeable team of sommeliers will be more than happy to help you choose the wine of the moment. On the food front, there's plenty of local cheese to try, from *çeçil* to Izmir Tulum, while chef Orhan Karademir prepares Italian-inspired boards and tapas, as well excellent bruschetta and pasta dishes. Plus, expect saxophone solo performances at the weekend.

vigneron-wine-house.business.site TEL +90 212 512 18 21

SIGARA

78 CZARNA OWCA WINE BAR

Dajwór 20/LU6, 31-052 Kraków, Poland

TO VISIT BEFORE YOU DIE BECAUSE

A welcome refuge for wine lovers in Kraków's historic centre, with a friendly and music-filled atmosphere

Czarna Owca's founders, Radek and Ida, were so inspired by the cosy, intimate wine bars they discovered during a trip to Verona that they decided to create one right here in their hometown of Kraków. Located in the city's atmospheric Kazimierz district, their bar offers a selection of wines from around the world, all picked by the duo themselves. As the owners say: 'We are a bit like a family, so we are not perfect. We learn every day and love talking to our guests.' Named after the proverbial black sheep, the bar is holding the fort in the middle of a beer country, with bottles by the likes of Subtilité wines from France's Touraine Chenonceaux region; Sassicaia by Tenuta San Guido in Tuscany (the only wine from a single wine estate in Italy to have its own DOC); and Oveja Negra—another black sheep, this time from Chile's Maule Valley. There are also excellent snacks, including pumpkin pesto on artisanal baguette from local suppliers such as the Nonna Maria's Bakery and Oliwki etc. delicatessen.

czarnaowcawinobar.pl TEL +48 576 446 088

79 ANTIGA LISBON

R. Santo António da Sé, 10, 1100-500 Lisbon, Portugal

TO VISIT BEFORE YOU DIE BECAUSE

A great selection of Portuguese wines, including great Vinho Verdes, natural wines and lovely local food

Located in the historical Alfama district, just around the corner from the cathedral, Antiga is a cosy and casual wine bar offering 40 different wines by the glass, from all the main winegrowing regions of Portugal. It offers natural and local sparkling wines as well as very small production bottles, but the wine to try first is a Vinho Verde. 'For two reasons: it's delicious and can only be found in Portugal,' says Antiga's Nathalia Dias. 'We have the Royal Palmeira, the royal highness of this type of wine. It is fresh and citric, but when you let it sit for a few minutes in the glass it grows secondary flavours of vanilla and toasted bread.' Other hits include the Elfa from Casa de Mouraz, with 30 grape varieties vinified simultaneously by Antonio Lopes Ribeiro, a master of natural and low-intervention wines in Portugal. The food menu is also worth a mention: dishes showcase Portuguese flavours and local ingredients such as seafood and black pork chorizo, with a sprinkling of Brazilian and African influences. Among the highlights are *alheira* cake ('the ultimate Portuguese comfort food'), salt-cured tuna from the Alentejo, and pork belly cooked with herbs and local sparkling wine.

antigawinebar.eatbu.com

TEL +351 927 262 738

80 CLUB DES CHÂTEAUX

R. Actor Taborda 43, 1000-007 Lisbon, Portugal

TO VISIT
BEFORE YOU DIE
BECAUSE

Created by a team of French and Portuguese winemakers, this bar aims to bring you closer to the producers

This unique wine bar in Lisbon's Saldanha district specialises in French and Portuguese wines direct from the producers. It belongs to 12 associated wineries, including the Portuguese Vieira de Sousa (Douro and Port Wines) and the French Domaine Bernard Haas (Alsace), Château Laballe (Armagnac), Château de Varennes (Beaujolais), Château Piron (Bordeaux), Château de Chamilly (Burgundy), Château Eugénie (Cahors), Champagne Bochet-Lemoine, Domaine Tour Saint Michel (Châteauneuf-du-Pape), Château d´Arlay (Jura), Château du Fresne (Loire) and Manoir de Grandouet (Normandy, organic cider and Calvados). Each has a long history (d'Arlay has been in the same family for over a 1,000 years) and is worth sampling, along with a French cheese platter, a classic duck confit or beef bourguignon. 'People in Portugal used to think that French wine was expensive, and we had to change this,' says Xavier Boyreau, founder and partner of Club des Châteaux. 'Every Wednesday we organise a tasting session dedicated to one winery, and the prices are aligned with the concept.' There are over 50 wines and spirits by the glass (prices start at €3.50), with smaller 7cl tasting glasses also available so you can try as many wines as you want.

chateaux.pt TEL +351 21 357 1351

81 MOVIA

Mestni trg 2, 1000 Ljubljana, Slovenia

TO VISIT
BEFORE YOU DIE
BECAUSE

This tiny wine bar gets all the big stuff right, from the warm welcome to the excellent selection of Slovenian wines

Hidden away in a little covered courtyard just beneath Ljubjana Castle, Movia is a cosy, atmospheric place with a few bar stools, a row of fine bottles, a vaulted ceiling, and a large terrace that is used in the summer. It is owned by one of the country's top winemakers, Aleš Kristančič, whose family business, the iconic Movia Winery in Goriška Brda, has been producing biodynamic orange wines and top-quality natural wines for decades. The winery has been internationally recognised for its excellent sparkling, white, red and macerated wines, all of which you can try here, along with a great selection of Slovenian natural wines by various producers. Slovenia is particularly known for its orange wines, from winemakers including Svetlik, Renčel, Radikon and... Movia, of course. Also on offer here are local delicacies, such as excellent olives, honey and Mlekarna Planika cheese, and even some Slovenian oysters and champagne.

movia.si/en/wine-bar TEL +386 51 304 580

82 LES 110 DE TAILLEVENT

16 Cavendish Sq., London W1G 9DD, UK

TO VISIT
BEFORE YOU DIE
BECAUSE

The clue is in the name: there are 110 wines by the glass to be sampled here in the foodie heaven that is Marylebone

Located in the former Coutts Bank on Cavendish Square, this chic bar and restaurant offers modern French cuisine and 110 wines by the glass. Designed by Pierre-Yves Rochon, its interiors feature bottle-green walls and frescos of vineyard landscapes. As for its cellar, it holds over 2,000 bottles, with wines dating back to 1897, while each by-the-glass reference is specially selected to be paired with seasonally inspired dishes. The accent here is on French wines, with Burgundy wines a perennial favourite. Head sommelier Imre Somogyi ensures that the wine programme features both big names and small producers, keeping the list one of the most unique in London, while chef Roxanne Lange prepares classics including spelt lobster risotto, Cornish turbot with Monalisa potato and tarte Tatin. Each dish of the six-course tasting menu can be enjoyed with a choice of four wines by the glass.

 les-110-taillevent-london.com TEL 020 3141 6016

83 NEWCOMER

5 Dalston Lane, London E8 3DF, UK

TO VISIT
BEFORE YOU DIE
BECAUSE

Newcomer has the best Austrian wine list in London, in a welcoming spot just off busy Dalston Junction

Newcomer Wines started out in 2014 selling Austrian wines from a tiny shop in Boxpark Shoreditch. Two years later, owners Peter Honegger and Daniela Pillhofer opened this bar and shop in Dalston, and are now sourcing natural wines from close to 100 growers across Central Europe. 'Our growers share a common purpose: to make wines that are an honest reflection of the place and the people that make them, leaving as little imprint and re-establishing biodiversity on the natural world as they go,' say the founders. According to manager Harry East, top sellers include the cult favourites such as Christian Tschida (Austria), Claus Preisinger (Austria), Domaine Matassa (France) and Agricola Foradori (Italy). Smaller, lesser-known producers featured are Raphaëlle Guyot (France), Wasenhaus (Germany), Selvadolce (Italy) and Markus Ruch (Switzerland). The weekly rotating by-the-glass wines are best enjoyed in the small leafy garden with a plate of potato sourdough and butter. Events include monthly tasting sessions with visiting winemakers, and there are plans for pop-ups and pairing experiences.

newcomerwines.com TEL +44 20 7249 2177

84 GORDON'S WINE BAR

7 Villiers St, London WC2N 6NE, UK

TO VISIT BEFORE YOU DIE BECAUSE

A London institution, this family business near Covent Garden is the place for a great glass of wine and a British cheese platter

For over 130 years, Londoners have enjoyed a chinwag and Chablis at Gordon's Wine Bar near Charing Cross Station. Its central location and historic interiors make it the perfect spot to meet up. In the summer, you can easily spot its Burgundy façade and long terrace along the Victoria Embankment, but even if the sun is shining, make sure to step inside and discover a vaulted, candlelit cellar with old oak barrels, black-and-white photos and newspaper clippings on the walls. Thought to be the oldest wine bar in London, Gordon's was established in 1890 and is still very much a family affair, with a long-serving, dedicated team overseen by Simon Gordon. Most wines are available by the glass, while among the current favourites are the house Bordeaux; a selection of natural wines; and a smooth Portuguese red called the Smiling Donkey. They can be paired with cheese, charcuteries, vegetarian and vegan sharing boards (the British platter features homemade Scotch egg, a pork pie and Stilton cheese). Featuring five wines historically linked to the bar and five specially paired cheeses, the '130 Years Cheese and Wine Pairing for Two' is always very popular.

gordonswinebar.com TEL +44 20 7930 1408

SPECIMEN
LUIS GORDON
& SONS LTD.
SOLE CONCESSIONAIRES
OF
ESTATE WINE

GORDON'S WINE BAR
Luis Gordon
SPECIALS REDS
* CHILE £24.60
Morande Reserva Pinot-Noir
* ITALY £21.00
Negroamaro IGP Salento
* FRANCE £28.50
Haut-Médoc 2007
* SPAIN £22.00
Terra-Alta Syrah-Garnacha-Carignan 2014
A DAY OF SMILES
CORONATION

85 NOBLE ROT WINE BAR & RESTAURANT

51 Lamb's Conduit St, London WC1N 3NB, UK

TO VISIT BEFORE YOU DIE BECAUSE

Everyone is welcome at this temple to good wine and good food in a historic Bloomsbury townhouse

Noble Rot started out in 2013 as a 'cork-popping, gut-busting, genre-disrupting' magazine about wine, food and the creative arts. In 2015, the team rolled up their sleeves and launched their very own bar and restaurant in Bloomsbury. It was quickly followed by a Soho outpost, with a Mayfair opening in the works. The original Noble Rot, located in an 18th-century townhouse, has been recognised for its inclusive and inspiring 30-page wine list, which ranges from undervalued wines by the glass to rare mature bottles from great estates. 'There's no room for any kind of wine-wankery here,' proudly say the Noble Rot founders, Dan Keeling and Mark Andrew, the duo behind importers Keeling Andrew & Co and Shrine to the Vine wine shop. It's all great stuff, and we've not even mentioned the food. Executive chef is Stephen Harris of The Sportsman, Britain's best gastropub, and his 'Franglais' menu features dishes such as Comté beignets with pickled walnut ketchup, slipsole with smoked butter and Dorset snails, garlic and parsley butter.

noblerot.co.uk TEL +44 20 7242 8963

7 FUENTES

86 SAGER + WILDE

193 Hackney Rd, London E2 8JL, UK

TO VISIT BEFORE YOU DIE BECAUSE

An eclectic wine list full of real discoveries, to be enjoyed in a beautifully refurbished pub – the British Lion – in east London

Sommelier Michael Sager got the wine bug while living in San Francisco, working under award-winning sommelier Raj Parr. He launched Sager + Wilde as a pop-up wine bar in Shoreditch in 2012, before settling down for good a year later in this old pub on the Hackney Road. Dating from 1859, the historic pub has been transformed into a cool venue with a bar topped with a cast-iron pavement light, and backlit wire wine racks on the walls. The award-winning bar focuses on low-intervention, organic and biodynamic wines, from both veteran and new-generation producers, mostly from Europe. The skins/orange section includes over 30 bottles, from Maurer Oszkár's Crazy Lúd from Serbia, to Andreas Tscheppe's Goldmuskateller Schwalbenschwanz from Austria. On the drinks list there are also interesting spirits such as Mezcal and Fernet, beer from the Jura region of France, and chef-driven low-alcohol ferments from the likes of Noma and Mugaritz. Foodwise, expect seasonal small plates and signature cheese toasties.

sagerandwilde.com

TEL +44 20 8127 7330

87 SEARCY'S CHAMPAGNE BAR

St Pancras, St Pancras International Station,
London N1C 4QL, UK

TO VISIT BEFORE YOU DIE BECAUSE

Europe's longest champagne bar, this is the place to enjoy a bit of armchair travelling, watching the trains go by

London's St Pancras Station is best known for the grand Gothic Revival hotel that fronts it on the busy ring road. But step inside and go up the steps to the Grand Terrace to take in another wonder of Victorian engineering: William Henry Barlow's single-span arched train shed, constructed of iron and glass. Just there, next to the Eurostar platforms and Tracey Emin's neon artwork, is a champagne bar managed by the UK's oldest caterer, Searcys, founded in 1847. Take a seat in a plush velvet booth, designed to evoke the feel of a traditional train carriage, and press the button for champagne. There are over 50 bottles on the menu, from Searcys own range, to bubbles by Drappier, Lanson and Veuve Clicquot. Also on offer are about 20 wines by the glass, plus Tokaji, Sauternes and Moscatel dessert wines. There's also a huge selection of seafood, from rock and native oysters, to Scottish salmon tartare and hand-dived Orkney scallop ceviche, and the option to stay for a British afternoon tea served in a bespoke suitcase stand.

stpancrasbysearcys.co.uk

TEL +44 20 7870 9900

88 NOSCH

24 rue Palais Grillet, 69002 Lyon, France

TO VISIT
BEFORE YOU DIE
BECAUSE

A wine bar and bistro in the historic centre of Lyon where every ingredient and bottle is sourced with care and passion

Wine and food go hand in hand in Lyon, the French capital of gastronomy. And this is nowhere more apparent than at Nosch, a friendly little wine bistro in Les Cordeliers. It is the passion project of Noémie Schmider, a graduate of the city's Paul Bocuse Institute, who started from scratch and opened her own place in 2018. The wine list focuses on Beaujolais and Burgundy, with sparkling wines such as Céline et Laurent Tripoz's Crémant de Bourgogne Brut; a Bourgogne Aligoté white wine by Sylvain Pataille; Domaine Duband's Nuits-Saint-Georges Pinot Noir, and La Bonne Tonne Beaujolais. There are also a few bottles from the nearby Coteaux du Lyonnais, and labels from farther afield, including Alsace, Savoie, and even Austria and Georgia. All are kept in a beautiful stonewall cellar. The wine by-the-glass selection changes weekly, while the menu is full of French classics, from a Rosette de Lyon platter and *paupiettes de veau* to the 'diet-buster' that is the lemon tartelette.

nosch.fr TEL +33 4 78 42 08 31

89 LA CAVE CAFÉ TERROIR

5 rue Montcharmont, 69002 Lyon, France

TO VISIT BEFORE YOU DIE BECAUSE

Sample the best of local fare from the Rhône Valley and beyond at this wine cellar linked to one of Lyon's top bistros

Hailing from one of Lyon's fine-dining dynasty, young chef Jeff Têtedoie is known for his passion for the gastronomy of the Auvergne-Rhône-Alpes region, best showcased at his bistrot-rôtisserie Café Terroir. He is also an oenophile, and this is where La Cave Café Terroir comes in. Located just around the corner from the main restaurant, this wine bar holds 1,200 wine references, as well as a beautiful cellar complete with an ageing tank. The wine list is focused on the Rhône Valley and offers a flight for almost every winery, with producers such as Jean-Michel Stephan or Alain Graillot represented. Come for an *apéro* from 6 to 7.30pm and you'll be able to sample appetisers such as homemade terrine and soft-boiled eggs with Beaufort little soldiers. Stay on, and you'll be offered not only the wines, but the full Terroir menu, with dishes such as asparagus, morilles and *vin jaune*, roast Bresse chicken and pink praline tartelette. It really is the best of both worlds.

en.cafeterroir.fr TEL +33 9 52 52 51 38

90 DE VINOS

C. de la Palma, 76, 28015 Madrid, Spain

TO VISIT
BEFORE YOU DIE
BECAUSE

This charming old-school bar may be in a time warp in terms of interiors, but its wine list is up to the minute

Located in a former grocery store in Madrid's Conde Duque neighbourhood, De Vinos has all the features of a classic Spanish space, from the hydraulic tiles on the floor, to the marble bar complete with coat hooks, and the walls lined with bottles of wines from around the country. Owner and sommelier Yolanda Morán is here to help you choose the perfect bottle from a selection of little-known denominations of origin and constantly evolving labels. Recently on the wine list were the likes of Grenabar by L'Octavin/Alice Bouvot from Jura, Vinista by Pedro Parra from Chile, and a Chenin Blanc by South Africa's Fram Wines. There are also special tasting sessions based on specific regions such as Jura, Beaujolais or Cordoba's Montilla-Moriles DOP. The accompanying selection of cheeses, Iberian meats and cured tuna are definitely not an afterthought, but a beautifully presented selection served in the traditional way, with various pickles, preserves and salted meats.

facebook.com/vinos.devinos

TEL +34 911 82 34 99

91 BERRIA

Pl. de la Independencia, 6, 28001 Madrid, Spain

TO VISIT
BEFORE YOU DIE
BECAUSE

The perfect terrace to sample fine vintages and fine dishes in Madrid's busiest district

Boasting a lovely terrace on Madrid's Plaza de la Independencia, Berria offers a long al fresco tasting session thanks to a dizzying choice of bottles: there are 3,500 different labels, including old vintages and rarities, and more than 100 wines by the glass that rotate every two weeks. 'We also have a section called Dunas de Berria,' explains wine director Tomás Ucha Altamirano. 'These are very exclusive wines, difficult to find on the market or too expensive to consume by the bottle, so we give you the opportunity to try them.' A team of seven sommeliers work and travel together to make sure they select the best wines for Berria. They also create experiences, picking rare wines for which a bespoke menu is created. The gastronomic offering is designed by renowned chef Juanjo López. 'A must at Berria,' continues Ucha Altamirano, 'is a plate of Santoña anchovies from Cantabria with a glass of Jacques Lassaigne champagne, or our brioche with Iberian dewlap and caviar combined with a glass of Domaine Roulot Auxey-Duresses.'

berriawinebar.com TEL +34 664 86 43 22

92 VINOLOGY

C. del Conde de Aranda, 11, 28001 Madrid, Spain

TO VISIT
BEFORE YOU DIE
BECAUSE

Just a few steps from the Retiro Park, this is a gem of a wine bar that will help you discover Spanish wines in all their variety

Born in Mendoza, Argentina, the daughter and granddaughter of winemakers, Pilar Oltra initially continued the family business, achieving great success by working around the world, making wine from the USA to France. She then became a sommelier, trained for a Master of Wine in London, and offered a myriad of tastings and courses. In 2021, she opened her first wine bar, Vinology, in Madrid's Salamanca neighborhood, 'to promote wine culture in an accessible way and pay tribute to the diversity of Spanish wine'. Designed as a homely space with cosy corners and elegant lighting (there is also a private space for tastings and other events in the basement), Vinology offers wines from all over the country, from Cádiz and Alicante, to Catalonia, Galicia and the Canary Island, and each wine is listed with the name of its producer. The market fresh cuisine includes seasonal dishes such as autumn salad with roasted pumpkin, and a smoked fish platter served with caviar and crème fraîche.

vinology.wine

TEL +34 916 91 72 38

BADIOLA

93 VOILA VÉ

100 Blvd Chave, 13005 Marseille, France

TO VISIT BEFORE YOU DIE BECAUSE

This vibrant neighbourhood bar captures Marseille's energy and taste for natural wines

Opened by Alix Huguet and Victor Million-Rousseau just before the COVID-19 pandemic, this bright bar in Marseille's Camas district is named after the local phrase for 'look here'. And we definitely do want to look at it very carefully; the colourful façade pulls you into a welcoming space that spills onto the pavement terrace at the front, just next to the tramway tracks, and stretches into a secluded patio at the back. Peer at its wine list and you will find only organic, biodynamic and natural wines such as Domaine Matrot's L'Effrontée and Domaines des Blaquières's Marius. 'Our goal is to make sure our guests do not feel self-conscious when faced with the world of wine that is sometimes too elitist,' explains Alix. The menu is split into three separate sections, all suited to different types of weather, time of the day or even mood. 'The Thirst-Quenchers' are light wines of any colour or origin; 'The Appetising' are slightly more complex wines perfect to enjoy with small bites; and 'The Gourmands' are tannic reds and opulent whites to pair with a more substantial dish, such as a baked Camembert with honey or a tarte Tatin.

barvoilave.com TEL +33 7 65 65 48 88

94 CIZ CANTINA E CUCINA

Viale Premuda, 44, 20129 Milan, Italy

TO VISIT
BEFORE YOU DIE
BECAUSE

This sommelier-led trattoria boasts a friendly team, hearty dishes and a dictionary-sized wine list

Named after its founder, sommelier Vincenzo 'Ciz' Gautieri, this small trattoria lets wine play a leading role: its wine list includes over 1,700 references (most of them natural or biodynamic), and at over 70 pages long, it makes for a riveting read. There's a focus on Italian and French wines (favourites include Rinaldi, Cantina Mascarello Bartolo and Clos Rougeard), but most countries are featured, from Hungary to Lebanon. Among the French labels are a couple of beautifully named gems, such as Le Gras C'est La Vie (loosely translating as 'fat is the best') by Famille de Boel in the northern Rhône; and a bottle of Fouzy Tout (meaning: 'put everything in it') by La Ferme du Plateau in the Loire Valley. You'll find the same infectious fun and good vibes from Gautieri's team, who will welcome you with trademark Italian hospitality. The kitchen is certainly not an afterthought: the food is simple but delicious and includes house specials such as spaghetti with cheese, pepper and mint; grilled octopus with chickpea purée; and classics such as saffron risotto and Milanese cutlet.

cizcantinaecucina.it

TEL +39 02 2318 9915

95 TANNICO

Via Savona 17, 20144 Milan, Italy

TO VISIT
BEFORE YOU DIE
BECAUSE

It has all the Italian wines you could ever wish for in a great space on Milan's hip via Savona

Part of the Tannico wine empire (which is said to be the most efficient and largest Italian online shop in the world), this elegant wine bar was founded by Juliette Bellavita in the heart of Milan's design district. It offers great seasonal food, such as small plates of meatballs in tomato sauce, creamed cod and crispy polenta, and tiramisu. However, the real draw is the amazing selection of wines at great prices. The list is far too long to go through in detail, but includes all the usual wines and more, from Alsatian bubblies to Slovenian orange wines and Austrian *pét na*t. Obviously the Italian selection is very thorough, with labels from the Dolomites (Pranzegg) to Puglia (Masseria Borgo dei Trulli). As for the constantly updated wine by the glass selection, it includes helpful tasting notes. For example, a Barbaresco DOCG Rabaja 2019 by Giuseppe Cortese is 'tannic, structured, territorial', while a Vino Bianco T by Francesco Guccione is 'mineral, savoury, floral'. Thirsty for more? You can also visit the Tannico Wine Corner in Milan's Mercato Centrale food court for more excellent wines and cheese boards.

tannicowinebar.it

TEL +39 02 0994 6657

96 ENOTECA INTERNAZIONALE

Via Roma, 62, 19016 Monterosso al Mare SP, Italy

TO VISIT BEFORE YOU DIE BECAUSE

The oldest wine shop in the historic centre of Monterosso, this quaint *enoteca* is the place to sample Cinque Terre wines

The Barbieri family's bustling *enoteca* offers a window into the wonderful local produce of Cinque Terre, starting with its wines. Its outstanding selection includes over 500 wines, many from the small local producers of the notoriously difficult to cultivate Cinque Terre DOC. The two typical wines are a dry white wine and a dessert wine made from dried grapes called Sciacchetrà, and they can be sampled together in a special tasting. There are also bigger names from the rest of Italy (Chianti, Barolo, Nebbiolo and Sassicaia) and around the world (mostly from California, South Africa and Australia). Sommeliers Valentina and Susy also guard some rare and precious wines reserved for connoisseurs, and offer wine tastings to all. The menu showcases the best of local products, from extra-virgin olive oil to Monterosso's salted anchovies, both of which are used to produce a delicious bruschetta. The deli section offers a great selection of cheese and cold meats, so you could grab a bottle and a picnic and head to the beach.

enotecainternazionale.com

TEL +39 0187 817278

97 BAR MURAL

Theresienstraße 1, 80333 Munich, Germany

TO VISIT
BEFORE YOU DIE
BECAUSE

Eat local and drink natural at this hip little bar with top-quality wines and Bib Gourmand food

Bar Mural is cooler and more laid-back than its big brother, the Michelin-starred restaurant of the same name (housed in the Museum of Urban and Contemporary Art and revered for its seasonal and vegan dishes). Bar Mural is located just to the north, in the Maxvorstadt university district, and follows a clear credo: 'Eat local. Drink natural.' Its founders are the award-winning duo Moritz Meyn and Wolfgang Hingerl – the latter being one of the most influential and progressive sommeliers in Germany. If you can, grab a seat at the bar counter (there is also a lovely courtyard terrace) to sample over 400 labels (there are over 1,000 references on the wine list) which include many natural wines, but also well-known winemakers from France, Italy and Slovenia. Germany is represented by winemakers such as Gabriel Scheuermann, Wasenhaus, Trossen and Konni & Evi. The tiny 5m² kitchen produces best-selling three to five course menus, while there are also local bread, cheese and ham platters to enjoy.

barmural.com TEL +49 89 27373380

98 RADEGAST

Nordre gate 2, 0551 Oslo, Norway

TO VISIT
BEFORE YOU DIE
BECAUSE

This riverside wine bar celebrates small female winemakers, and is also worth a visit for its unique setting and summer terrace

To find this hidden wine bar, you will have to stroll through Grünerløkka, a cosy neighborhood full of independent shops and eateries, and head straight to the old whitewashed manor house by the river, also home to the Nedre Foss Gård restaurant. Here, you will find a welcoming space—named after the Slavic god of strength, honour and hospitality—lined with bottle-filled cabinets. 'We buy what we like, and we have a weak spot for small, female winemakers, or winemakers that love what they do, rather than just doing it for the money,' explains sommelier Christina Mari Helle. 'So, our wine selection of over 800 wines ranges from the funkiest natural wines to classic producers from Burgundy. We open almost everything by the glass.' In winter, snacks include a great selection of Norwegian cheese (as well as classics from France and Switzerland), but the place comes alive in the summer, with a huge outdoor terrace opened for lunch and dinner. Tasting sessions are held throughout the year on Wednesdays and Fridays.

nedrefossgaard.no/radegast TEL +47 92 33 82 93

99 NEKTAR

Fredensborgveien 42, 0177 Oslo, Norway

TO VISIT BEFORE YOU DIE BECAUSE

Discover an incredible range of champagne and other fine French wines in this quaint corner of Oslo

Established by local wine and hospitality veteran Veslemøy Hvidsten, this family-run bar is full of character. Perched on a gently sloping street in Olso's historic centre, it is located in a traditional red timber-clad house dating from 1814. Its wine list is based on sustainability and quality, with a focus on small producers from Champagne, Loire, Jura and Burgundy. 'We always have 15-20 wines by the glass and very often we can open something in addition to that if there is reasonable demand for it,' explains sommelier Matija Kolar. 'We change all the wines every week to keep our customers and ourselves entertained.' The list also includes labels from Germany and unusual bottles such as I am Not a Big Wine by Milan Nestarec in the Czech Republic, or Revenge of the Crayfish by South Africa's Sakkie Mouton. Head chef Edward Shaw serves up a seasonal menu featuring locally grown ingredients, as well as best-selling dishes such as anchovies on toast, halloumi fries and mac and cheese.

nektarvinbar.no TEL +47 91 92 44 46

100 VIN BJØRVIKA

Operagata 11, 0194 Oslo, Norway

TO VISIT
BEFORE YOU DIE
BECAUSE

Sample one of the world's best wine lists and take in Oslo's incredible waterfront transformation

Facing Snohetta's iceberg-like Opera House and located next to the stooping Munch Museum in the Oslo Bay Area, Vin Bjørvika is surrounded by contemporary glass-wall architecture. Inside, however, it's another story, with a cosy space dedicated to the best wines from around the world. At any given time, there are over 100 by-the-glass wines to try, while its wine cellar contains around 10,000 bottles with 1,800 different wines. In September 2022, it was awarded the prestigious World's Best Wine Bar List by World of Fine Wine, so there's only good stuff here, including a rarely seen English Roebuck Rosé de Noirs, and bottles by the South African pioneer of Chenin Blanc, Ken Forrester. Sit back, watch the sun set over the harbour, and enjoy a cheese platter with a glass of Chardonnay, or a lobster soup with a glass of champagne, before digging into the wonderful selection of labels. Bonus points if you manage to taste some of the 100 different gins on offer.

vin-bjorvika.no

101 FERRAMENTA

Piazza Giovanni Meli, 8, 90133 Palermo, Italy

TO VISIT
BEFORE YOU DIE
BECAUSE

This hotspot for oenophiles and gourmets is located in a historical pallazo dating to 1600, which creates a unique atmosphere

Just around the corner from Palermo's landmark San Domenico church is a jumble of little alleyways worth exploring. On a small square you will find Ferramenta, a wine bar and restaurant housed in Palazzo Pantelleria, a historic building dating from 1600 (in which you can stay by the way). Opened in 2018, it has very quickly become a hotspot for oenophiles and gourmets thanks to its sprawling outdoor terrace and ace team of sommeliers who, unsurprisingly, love nothing more than to go on research trips, especially to Champagne (they brought back some De Souza and Bruno Paillard). Their wine list includes bottles from Sicily's Eudes and Graci wineries, Abruzzo's Torre dei Beati and Piedmont's Fontanafredda. Snack on some *panelle* fritters or the house platter (fried cheese, *sfincione*, sausage pizza, fries and bruschetta), or opt for any of chef Ivan Spitaleri's beautifully presented seasonal dishes such as tagliatelle with cream of broad beans and mussels. To top it all off, there's also some excellent cocktails.

@ferramentapalermo

TEL +39 392 513 7716

102 LA SANG

Carrer d'Antoni Frontera, 24, 07004 Palma, Balearic Islands, Spain

TO VISIT BEFORE YOU DIE BECAUSE

Discover natural wines and new Mallorcan classics in this simple space run a by a dynamic duo

Opened in 2019 by young couple Lukas Lundgren and Eritrea Willoughby, Bar La Sang takes its name from its first address, a small corner space on Costa de la Sang St. Pioneers of the natural wine scene in Mallorca, the pair spent lockdowns delivering wine across town, before attracting crowds and being named one of the top natural wine bars in Spain. It has since moved to bigger premises, now with a kitchen helmed by chef Diego Silva, and has developed into a company importing wine from the mainland. Here, you can learn all about Majorcan varieties, including Manto Negre, Callet and Fogoneu, and sample the creations of local producers such as Solviellas Sisters, Hada Furthmann and Jaume Prats. The energetic team organises regular pop-ups (featuring chefs such as Gareth Storey and Jakub Baster) and tasting sessions of wines by the likes of Moritz Kissinger and Corentin Houillon. Last year they also set up the island's first natural wine fair, Poc a Poc, with VIP guests, including Austria's Christian Tschida and Spain's Barranco Oscuro.

@barlasang TEL +34 645 59 13 93

103 AVANT COMPTOIR DE LA MER

3 Carrefour de l'Odéon, 75006 Paris, France

TO VISIT BEFORE YOU DIE BECAUSE

If you can get a spot inside, it's the place for a French *apéro* with a glass of chilled white wine and a plate of seafood

Sit at the long counter of this bar in busy Odéon—you'll need to be lucky, there are only about ten stools and then it's standing only—and look around: the menu hangs above your head, and the walls are lined with chilled glass cabinets holding bottle after bottle of delicious wines. It is one of the many great ideas of French celebrity chef Yves Camdeborde, known for his bistronomy establishments (best described as the French equivalent of the UK's gastropubs). Here, you can catch up with friends over a drink and a selection of seafood-based small plates, from Bloody Mary oysters, tuna tartare, mussels, ceviche or cod beignets with lime. There are about 1,000 bottles of wine, which you can taste before ordering. Among the regulars on the wine list are Happy Hours by Domaine Charles Hours, Galinette by Domaine de Sulauze, La Begou de Maxime Magnon and Le Chenin by Catherine et Pierre Breton. There's also a couple of other comptoirs nearby focusing on meaty small plates.

camdeborde.com/les-restaurants/avant-comptoir-de-la-mer

TEL +33 1 42 38 47 55

104 228 LITRES

3 rue Victor Massé, 75009 Paris, France

TO VISIT BEFORE YOU DIE BECAUSE

A showstopping selection of natural wines and champagnes in the heart of Pigalle

Founded by Pierre Renauld in 2018, this cosy and relaxed Parisian bar features beautiful interiors designed to reflect the different materials used in the winemaking process, including wood and stainless steel. Holding over 600 references, 228 Litres specialises in natural wines and champagne, served with seasonal sharing plates. 'We particularly love Jean-Baptiste Semmartin's Jurançon Sec, and the Petit Manseng and Gros Manseng from Lucq-de-Béarn' says Renauld, whose unusual selection also includes a *mousseux* from Jura's Bruno Bienaimé; a Sans Soufre Blanc from Japan's Takeda Winery and a Île de Beauté Burghese by Corsica's Sant Armettu. Business is booming and Renauld has now joined forces with his brother Louis and friends Maxime Al Bitar and Robin Lenfant. Every month, the team welcomes a new chef-in-residence; past guests have included Noé Lazare and La Jacquardise. What's more, you can shop to your heart's content in the team's adjoining bottle shop, La Cave Pigalle.

228litres.fr

TEL +33 1 71 60 51 57

La Joue

105 LEGRAND FILLES & FILS

4 rue des Petits-Champs, 75002 Paris, France

TO VISIT
BEFORE YOU DIE
BECAUSE

This historic address near the Palais-Royal is known for its incredible setting and expert selection of French wine

This Parisian *caviste* and restaurant is full of history: not only is it located in the Galerie Vivienne, a covered arcade dating from 1823, it is also here that Lucien Legrand pretty much started the wine merchant business. Until the 1970s, wine was bought in crates from Bercy, the world's largest wine market, but Lucien decided to go and meet the winemakers, selecting the wines himself and launching the Sélection Legrand. It is a family tradition that continues to this day, with the team now travelling around the world to select wines. The full list includes 10,000 unique references, each celebrating a particular terroir. Besides French wines, there are handful of wines from the USA (Arnot Roberts), Italy (Occhipinti) and Greece (Economou). Sit at a table in the *vinothèque*, or on the terrace in the *galerie*, and enjoy a glass of Château Angélus or Domaine Saint Andrieu paired with the Asian-inflected French cuisine of chef Benjamin Anthoni.

caves-legrand.com TEL +33 1 42 60 07 12

106 WILLI'S WINE BAR

13 rue des Petits-Champs, 75001 Paris, France

TO VISIT BEFORE YOU DIE BECAUSE

Despite its founder's best efforts, Willi's has grown up and turned into a true Parisian institution

Who better than an Englishman in Paris to turn the local wine scene upside down and upset the status quo? That's what happened when Mark Williamson (who, learned his trade from the late British wine merchant Steven Spurrier, who organised the famous Judgment of Paris) opened Willi's Wine Bar in 1980 by the Jardin du Palais Royal. As an outsider, he did what he pleased, ignoring the strict French edicts, focusing on 'frequently interesting, sometimes obscure, invariably gorgeous wines'. He started by serving Rhône wines when no one else was doing it, and over the years he has built an eclectic and surprising wine list, full of unique discoveries, 'with a special mention today for producers from the Mosel, Douro and Piedmont'. These can be enjoyed with French bistro fare such as crispy roasted guineafowl and bitter chocolate terrine, surrounded by wonderful posters by contemporary artists, specially commissioned by Willi's.

willliswinebar.com TEL +33 1 42 61 05 09

107 LAVINIA VICTOR HUGO

22 av. Victor Hugo, 75116 Paris, France

TO VISIT
BEFORE YOU DIE
BECAUSE

The largest wine shop in Paris is also a bar that caters to every taste and budget

After closing down its historic Madeleine store, leading European wine distributor and retailer Lavinia opened its flagship store and bar in 2021 on a grand avenue near the Champs-Elysées. Although it is surrounded by four-star hotels and luxury boutiques, it offers a wide selection of wines for every budget. It stocks over 6,500 wines from 30 different countries, over 1,000 of which can be enjoyed at the bar, along with cheese and charcuterie platters. Among the wines available to sample here are bottles by the likes of Clos Rougeard, Vincent Dauvissat and Domaine Tempier, as well as a very detailed selection of champagnes, all at fair prices. The expert sommeliers, Nicolas Chimot and William Simeray, organise tastings and wine producer visits, and watch over the basement cellar filled with over 400 grands crus and millésimes by producers such as Mouton-Rothschild, Peyre Rose and Anselme Selosse.

lavinia.com/fr-fr/caves/lavinia-victor-hugo TEL +33 1 42 97 20 20

GAJA

108 CAPELA INCOMUM

79-81, Travessa do Carregal 77, 4050-167 Porto, Portugal

TO VISIT
BEFORE YOU DIE
BECAUSE

An atmospheric bar in central Porto that offers the chance to sample interesting local wines and port cocktails

Located in a 16th-century chapel, this unique bar features candlelit interiors (with the altarpiece the only remnant of the former chapel) and a tranquil paved courtyard. Both areas are great spaces in which to discover and taste a wide range of Portuguese wines. 'We like to create a relationship between us and our guests, by sharing information, talking about the wine and making them feel at home,' says owner Francisca Lobão, a Porto native, who is always searching for new 'outside the box' wines, between the classics and the new and organic. The wine list focuses mostly on the Douro and Minho regions, with the team of six on hand to provide backstories for each bottle. Also on offer are port wine cocktails and small sharing plates such as roasted black pudding with goat's cheese and pulled pork burgers. The top floor is used for wine tastings, poetry nights and writing clubs, so there's always something going on here.

capelaincomum.pt TEL +351 936 129 050

109 VINOTEKA SODČEK

Linhartov trg 8, 4240, Radovljica, Slovenia

TO VISIT BEFORE YOU DIE BECAUSE

Although it's off the beaten track, this charming bar is well worth a visit for its owners' vast knowledge of Slovenian wines

This family-run wine shop and bar opened in 1995 in the centre of Radovljica, a medieval town near the Julian Alps in northern Slovenia. It's the best place to rest and recuperate after a spot of sightseeing or hiking. Radovljica is best known for its honey and chocolate, but here at Sodček it's all about the wines. 'Slovenia is a European wine map in miniature,' say the owners, who offer guided wine tastings presenting the world of top Slovenian wines, paired with local prosciutto, cheese and olive oil. 'Each bottle is hand selected to delight our guests with unique and diverse wines from the three wine-growing regions of Slovenia, Primorje, Posavje and Drava. Founder Aleš Čebašek is a living encyclopedia on Slovenian wines, and among his selection are bottles such as a Malvazija Orange by Rokovi Vinogradi, a Penina Brut Zero by Ščurek and a Kapovolto by Movia.

vinoteka-sodcek.si

TEL +386 4 531 50 71

110 CUL SEC

61 rue de Cernay, 51100 Reims, France

TO VISIT
BEFORE YOU DIE
BECAUSE

Named after the French for 'down it!', this great neighbourhood wine bar is worth the trip to Cernay for its champagne selection

This fun 'cave à manger' offers great French food, including three types of *tourte* (pie) and various terrines by one of the country's top artisans, Bruno Herbin, and the house specialty, tartare. It also has a small but tempting selection of wines by the glass (including a Blanc de Blanc by JL Vergnon, a Viognier by Domaine de Montine and a Sancerre by Lucien Crochet). But you'll want to take some time to peruse the six-page strong champagne menu, which, of course, features all the big names (from Dom Pérignon and Krug to Ruinart and Bollinger) as well as lots of bottles by smaller producers such as Emmanuel Brochet, Yann and Séverine Alexandre and Waris-Hubert. There's also a wide selection of whites, reds and rosés from all over France, and a short but sweet 'carte de vins du monde' – in 2023 the list was voted one of France's top 100. Cul Sec is part of Reims' Maison Kikel group, which also owns a nearby restaurant, brasserie and pâtisserie.

culsec-reims.fr

TEL +33 3 26 03 36 63

111 ENOTECA BORTONE

Via di Monserrato, 4, 00186 Rome, Italy

TO VISIT
BEFORE YOU DIE
BECAUSE

This charming *enoteca* is the best place to sample local Lazio wines and have a taste of *la dolce vita*

There's no shortage of cute *enotece* in Rome; there's one on practically every corner. But we do have a soft spot for sommelier Patrizia Bortone's little wine bar near the bustling Campo de' Fiori, which opened its doors in 1996. Here, she works with her friend Stefania De Franceschi, and her son, Giampaolo Panei, a chef who selects the best local ingredients to serve up on lovely platters and in the delicatessen (including excellent olive oils and Pastalive products). Among Bartone's favourites are white wines grown on Etna's slopes, or the wines from Lazio, which 'are aromatic but not sweet'. 'I also like the red wines of seaside areas because they are a little bit salty, fruity and mineral,' she explains. 'But when I eat meat, I choose the big red wines, such as a Montepulciano, or my favourite: a Barbaresco from Piemonte, with its spicy notes.' Also on offer here are natural wines by La Cantina di Cunéaz in the Val d'Aosta and Reyter in South Tyrol, Castello Bonomi wines from Lombardia, and San Leonardo wines from the Dolomites.

enotecabortone.it

TEL +39 06 6880 4668

112 IL PICCOLO

Via del Governo Vecchio, 64-75, 00186 Rome, Italy

TO VISIT
BEFORE YOU DIE
BECAUSE

This classic Roman *enoteca* has been serving excellent wines by the glass for nearly 50 years

With its Baroque fountains and unique shape, Piazza Navona is one of Rome's most elegant sites. Not to be missed. And the same goes for the charming Il Piccolo just a short walk away. Make sure you complete your postcard-perfect tour of the capital by including a break at this charming little wine shop, established in 1980, and now run by Riccardo, the sommelier son of one of the original founders, Giancarlo Davoli. Inside it has about five tables and bottle-green wooden shelves lined with delicious bottles, and outside a row of tables neatly lined up in a tiny alleyway. It is always packed with regulars, but if you do find a spot to sit you will be rewarded with a selection of tasty *salumi* and cheese boards, small pasta dishes such as *cacio e pepe*, as well as around ten red and ten white wines by the glass. These include the likes of a Verdicchio from Le Marche or an Aglianico from Campania, as well as wines from the Lazio region.

@enoteca_il_piccolo TEL +39 06 6880 1746

LE PENDU DU RAISIN
MIRO
ROSA TERRA

113 FOU

2e Middellandstraat 8, 3021 BM Rotterdam, Netherlands

TO VISIT BEFORE YOU DIE BECAUSE

This welcoming bar and shop is the passion project of one of the country's top sommeliers

A former three Michelin-starred sommelier turned kitchen chef, Sigurd Snoeijs opened this wine bar, shop and restaurant at the beginning of 2021 in the Rotterdam-West area, where it is surrounded by a cool mix of shops and eateries. It has a large terrace at the front and warm brick-and-stone interiors. The shop follows the same schedule as the bar, which means you can still buy a bottle or two late at night. The wine list is built from a selection of around 400 wines of organic and biodynamic production and includes 250 natural wines, selected by specialist sommelier Ilya Mikhaylov, with big names such as Bini, Bouju, Matassa and Gravner. Also featured are classic winemakers such as Domaine Dujac and Comtes Lafon from Burgundy. Fou's specialty is a personal approach to wine and food matching and hospitality, says Snoejis. 'With a young and inspired team, we find new wines and think of new dishes every day.'

 wijnfou.nl TEL +31 6 11473231

114 GANBARA

C. de San Jerónimo 21, 20003 San Sebastián, Gipuzkoa, Spain

TO VISIT BEFORE YOU DIE BECAUSE

This typical Basque bar and restaurant is all about perfectly presented *pintxos* and carefully curated wines

A visit to San Sebastián and a stop at Ganbara should be at the top of any self-respecting gourmet's to-do list. Here, you can soak up the local tradition of eating elaborate and always delicious *pintxos* (Basque tapas) and drinking the slightly sparkling, dry white *txakoli* wine, which is poured from several feet high into a short cocktail glass to aerate the wine and release the bubbles. A local institution, Ganbara is a family bar and restaurant, established by José Ignacio Martínez and Amaia Ortuzar in 1984 and now run by their children (son Amaiur is in charge of the wine cellar). Sit at the ground-floor bar or at a barrel on the tiny terrace, and enjoy around 300 references from 40 different regions (the same list is available in the gastronomic restaurant downstairs). Try Guindilla peppers, spider crab tartlet or garlicky gambas with a glass of Bizkaiko/Getariako Txakolina or a Izar-Leku Brut Vintage, then carry on through the wine list which gathers great producers from all corners of the world.

ganbarajatetxea.com TEL +34 943 42 25 75

115 MAKU WEINBAR & CAFÉ

Ohligser Markt 1, 42697 Solingen, Germany

TO VISIT BEFORE YOU DIE BECAUSE

It's a friendly, casual spot to enjoy a carefully chosen selection of biodynamic and natural wines

This modern café and wine bar, located in the centre of Solingen, just north of Cologne, is an easy-going place that has something to offer all day long. In the mornings, it's a lovely café serving organic lemonades, specialty coffee and the best cinnamon buns in town. If you come for lunch or dinner, take your pick from 35 carefully selected bottles. 'Our wines are made exclusively from sustainable, organic or biodynamic wineries with whom we are in personal contact,' explains Sascha Novakovic, who set up Maku with his brother (they also own a restaurant and deli in town). 'Our bestseller is, of course, our house white wine—a Pinot Blanc made by Weingut Jürgen Leiner in Pfalz. Private bottling from rosé to red wine from across Europe complement our seasonally changing wine list.' Along with cold platters and daily specials, you can enjoy a The Flower and the Bee Ribeiro by Coto de Gomariz in Galicia, or a Kaiserstuhl Pinot Noir by Holger Koch in Baden.

makuconcept.com/weinbar

Holm
Holm
Holm
ceado

116 COMBO

Odengatan 52, 113 51 Stockholm, Sweden

TO VISIT BEFORE YOU DIE BECAUSE

An intimate, welcoming space with an award-wining wine list and great fuss-free food

Small and cosy, this wine bar, right opposite the landmark public library in Stockholm's Vasastan, sits only 24 inside. Although a little noisy, it's still the perfect place to huddle around a glass of wine. Its wine list (which won Star Wine List's Shortlist of the year 2022 in Sweden) contains about 200 wines—updated every day-all available either by the bottle or the glass. The list is organised by type of wine rather than country, with labels such as Domaine du Pélican (Jura), Giannitessari (Veneto) and Huia (New Zealand). Sommelier Jens Lundqvist (who founded PA & Co and Bistro Süd with his brother Niklas and friend Håkan Ericson) wanted to create a welcoming space, not just for oenophiles but for anyone wanting to taste something new. So they stock everything from affordable Sauvignon Blanc from southern France to Sine Qua Non by the glass. It's the same story with the food: made with love, but nothing too expensive—from risotto and beef bourguignon to chocolate cake.

 combovinbaren.com TEL +46 8 522 256 52

117 ALSACE À BOIRE

14 rue du 22 Novembre, 67000 Strasbourg, France

TO VISIT
BEFORE YOU DIE
BECAUSE

Discover a great variety of Alsatian wines a pretzel's throw away from picturesque Petite France

The clue is in the name: this wine shop and bar specialises in Alsatian drinks—mostly wines, but also beers and spirits. There are over 170 references, including 51 Alsatian grand crus, and a large selection of natural, organic, biodynamic and environmentally friendly wines. The friendly team of sommeliers help guests choose a bottle from the *vinothèque* (don't worry, it can be cooled down in six minutes), with current favourites including Domaine Mélanie Pfister's Pinot Gris, Domaine Eblin-Fuchs's Gewurztraminer Vendanges Tardives or a Terroir de Roche Riesling natural wine. Everything is beautifully listed and accompanied by tasting notes in a catalogue also available online. There are around 20 wines by the glass, including orange wines and *crémants* (tasting menus are also available), and a food menu featuring planchettes of local Munster and Bargkaas cheese, terrines and cold cuts. Visit on a Saturday to join one of their popular 'meet the winegrower' tasting sessions. So far over 70 producers have come to present their creations, from Pierre Wach to Katia Simonis.

alsaceaboire.fr TEL +33 3 90 00 21 61

118 DIE MOSEL

Rißbacher Str. 13, Dr. Ernst-Spies-Allee 5-6, 56841 Traben-Trarbach, Germany

TO VISIT BEFORE YOU DIE BECAUSE

This lovely bar and shop set in a former wine merchant's villa aims to showcase the best wines from the Moselle

A welcome addition to the Moselle's individual winery tasting rooms is this regional *vinothèque* and wine shop located in a neoclassical villa built in 1890 by wine merchant Richard Langguth. Featuring a large vaulted wine cellar, its Riesling Garden and a covered terrace with a postcard-perfect view of the river, it offers around 150 wines from the region, with approximately 25 wines and sparkling wines by the glass, by producers such as Rita und Rudi Trossen, Richard Scheid and Dr. Loosen (not to mention seasonal specials such as mulled wine and Federweisser). From the snake light installation on the floor to the bespoke wine racks made from vineyard poles, every detail here has been thought through with care and passion by owners Manuel (a former digital strategy manager and sixth-generation Traben-Trarbach wine trader) and his wife, Burcu Stolte, a hospitality expert. The sharing plate menu includes global hits such as *pimientos de Padrón*, *tonkatsu* and Sichuan beef salad.

shop-diemosel-wine.myshopify.com TEL +49 6541 8127688

MUSEUM

119 VINHO WINEBAR

Kuninkaankartanonkatu 8, 20810 Turku, Finland

TO VISIT BEFORE YOU DIE BECAUSE

Head to the oldest city in Finland to discover a highly praised selection of wines from around the world

Vinho Winebar was established only in 2019 but has already won many awards for its wine list, deemed 'very complete, with a really great selection of wines at good price points'. Located in Turku's central Martti district, the bar is a bright and airy space, with checkerboard floors, white walls and plenty of greenery. 'Our wine menu contains wines from all over the world including classics, but also less well-known ones,' say the owners Pietari Paakkola and Terhi Pihlaja. 'Our specialty is our tailor-made wine tastings: you can have your wine tasting whenever you want, choose the wines you desire, or ask for a total surprise.' There are 150 wines by the glass, including the likes of Inama Vulcaia Fumè or Château d'Yquem, as well as a selection of cheeses, charcuteries and vegan dishes. Despite all these assets, the true star of the show remains Vinho's wine-sniffing Dachshund Leni, who can spot a bad wine from a mile away.

vinho.fi TEL +358 10 2997610

120 TERRA À VINS

Carrer de Císcar 48, 46005 Valencia, Spain

TO VISIT BEFORE YOU DIE BECAUSE

If you manage to squeeze in here, you'll be rewarded the cream of the crop of Spanish wines

This pared-back space in Valencia's affluent La Gran Via district is the domain of Pablo Cavieres, a straight-talking wine enthusiast who is said to believe that, apart from a few exceptions, the only great Spanish wines hail from Galicia, the Canary Islands, Priorat and Jerez. So, forget about *riberitas* and *riojitas*, and take your pick from the excellent selection of sherries and bottles by winemakers such as Envinate, Venus de la Figuera, Viña de Martin Escolma and Bodeagas Tradición. Terra à Vins opened its doors in 2018, and has been eschewing food and travel journalists ever since. But word has got around that Pablo has plenty of stories to tell about every label, keeping you informed and entertained. And let's not forget the food: top-quality bar snacks from local bakery Le Roi, charcuterie from Madønado and hake cheeks from Alalunga. Terra a Vins might be tiny and hard to get into (with only nine seats and no bookings) but it sure packs a punch.

terraavins.com

TEL +34 960 08 18 55

121 VINO VERO

Fondamenta de la Misericordia, 2497, 30100 Venice, Italy

TO VISIT BEFORE YOU DIE BECAUSE

Have a Spritz by the Rialto, but then head straight to this gem for your fill of natural wines

We can't think of a more perfect setting to enjoy a glass of natural wine in Venice than on Vino Vero's terrace by the Misericordia canal in Cannaregio, one of the few areas in town that locals have not fully abandoned to tourists. Established in 2014 as the first wine bar in Venice dedicated exclusively to natural wine, Vino Vero offers a selection of over 600 labels to be tasted with its gourmet *cicchetti* (Venetian small bites such as cream of broccoli with *bleu di bufala*, blackberry mustard and walnut on bread). Founders Matteo Bartoli, his wife Mara Sartore and brother Massimiliano were partly inspired by their experience as partners in a biodynamic winery in Tuscany, but their young and international team of sommeliers is equally enthusiastic. Their latest finds include the Iliana Malihin winery in Greece, Philippe Pacalet in Bourgogne, Solenghi in Emilia-Romagna and Vino Riflesso in Piedmont. Make sure to try an Amarone della Valpolicella, Veneto's intensely flavoured red wine. Vino Vero also has an adjoining art gallery space and an outpost in Lisbon.

vinovero.wine/luoghi/venezia

TEL +39 041 275 0044

122 MAST

Porzellangasse 53, 1090 Vienna, Austria

TO VISIT
BEFORE YOU DIE
BECAUSE

This modern Viennese bar has quickly become a hangout for wine lovers thanks to its dynamic founding duo

Mast gets its name from the first two letters of each of its founders' first names, Matthias Pitra and Steve Breitzke. The pair of sommeliers spent over 15 years working at high-end restaurants before opening their wine bar in 2017. 'We don't want to be pigeonholed,' they say. 'But if you know our passion for wine, it's clear that organic is standard and the focus is on natural wines. We are also out and about a lot, walking through vineyards, tasting in the cellars, philosophising with the winegrowers.' Based on their personal tastes, this 'lovingly selected collection of fascinating people and passionate craftspeople' features around 1,300 organic and biodynamic labels, from Austria's Veyder-Malberg and France's Domaine Belluard to bigwigs like Christian Tschida. The pair has also brought in chef Lukas Lacina to prepare a seasonal, local menu which has just been rewarded a Green Star Bib Gourmand. Let Lacina surprise you with the Chef's Choice menu, or just come for a simple lunch of spinach and mountain cheese dumplings. Even better: Mast is also open on Sundays, which is quite rare in Austria, even in a big city like Vienna.

mast.wine

TEL +43 1 9226679

123 SOMM

Pylimo str. 21, 01141 Vilnius, Lithuania

TO VISIT
BEFORE YOU DIE
BECAUSE

Three of the country's top chefs and sommeliers have joined forces to open this excellent Spanish-inspired bar

Somm was set up in 2016 by three colleagues and friends: Egidijus Lapinskas, one of Lithuania's leading chefs, and Arminas Darasevičius and Narimantas Miežys, two of the country's best-known sommeliers. Painted in contrasting red and black with lots of wooden features and an angular white bar at the centre, Somm was inspired by the tapas bars found at the other end of Europe. Selected by a team of six sommeliers supervised by Miežys, managing director and Best Baltic Sommelier 2021, the wine list comprises 400 references. It covers not only classic winegrowing regions but also emerging countries including Georgia, Armenia and Lebanon. You will love the 'Wines by Sommelier' section, where the team reveals their favourite of the moment. Food is prepared fresh on the day, with dishes coming out of the wood-fired stove or brought straight to the tables in sizzling frying pans. There's also an assortment of sharing platters, smoked fish and tartares.

somm.lt TEL +370 684 64622

124 GRONO

Mokotowska 54, 00-538, Warsaw, Poland

TO VISIT
BEFORE YOU DIE
BECAUSE

A cool little bar in trendy Mokotowska that is not to be missed for its excellent selection and service

It won't come as a surprise that this beautifully designed wine bar and shop on Warwaw's fashionable Mokotowska belong to a highly successful hospitality group, Ferment, whose Michelin-starred Kieliszki na Próżnej restaurant is known for its perfect pairing of food and wine. A small but flowing open-plan space, Grono ('bunch' in Polish) was designed by Moszczyńska Puchalska with details such as arched alcoves, recalling the vaults of a wine cellar, and a floor inspired both by the city's modernist *gorseciki* mosaics and the colours of the limestone rocks in a vineyard. The wine list focuses on 'low-intervention, honest wines' by small family-run European wineries; all are opened by the glass, using Coravin for both still and sparkling wines. The team of young sommeliers is on hand to help you choose the perfect bottle to pair with your home-cooked dinner, or to open the latest Riesling or Tokaji for you. Bar snacks include truffle chips and cheeses from Włoski Mąż.

grono.waw.pl TEL +48 500 310 261

ZARATE

125 MOEVENPICK WEIN

Nüschelerstrasse 1, 8001 Zurich, Switzerland

TO VISIT BEFORE YOU DIE BECAUSE

A Swiss classic that offers a wide selection of Swiss and international wines, and boasts a walk-in rarity room

Everyone in Switzerland knows the Mövenpick brand, which has given its name to luxury hotels, delicious ice creams and a restaurant chain. However, not everyone knows that it is also a leading importer of great wines, and this wine bar and shop in central Zurich is its flagship. Its wine list comprises 500 wines from around the world, at pretty affordable prices for Switzerland, including some Swiss labels (Staatskellerei Zürich, Guido Brivio and Cave Fin Bec), always difficult to find abroad. Bottled wines can be purchased at the bar to take home at shop prices. There is a walk-in rarity room, and each year the team selects a wine of the year: the 2023 winner is 2019 Falling Blue D66 von Dave Phinney Maury, Languedoc-Roussillon. Regular events include free-flowing Champagne Pol Roger on Tuesdays and Big Bottle Fridays, when large bottles are uncorked and served by the glass. Favourite dishes include a classic beef tartare and *flammkuchen*.

moevenpick-wein.com/de/moevenpick-wein-bar-zuerich

TEL +41 44 211 91 39

126 CLOUD WINE

30 Sala Daeng 1 Alley, Silom, Bang Rak, Bangkok 10500, Thailand

TO VISIT BEFORE YOU DIE BECAUSE

This beautifully stocked wine bar and shop is a key tenant in a great new community space

This great little bottle shop and bar is located in the Commons Saladaeng, an innovative community space with cutting-edge architecture near Bangkok's Lumphini Park. And Cloud Wine is similarly forward-thinking: a pioneer of natural, organic and biodynamic wines in Bangkok, it offers '80 labels of artisanal wines made by individuals and families who care about their surroundings and sustainable farming practices'. It's a great showcase for Wine Garage, an outfit founded by sommelier Kim Wachtveitl, winemaker Philippe Bramaz and wine 'doctor' Guenther Forster, which has transformed the Bangkok scene. On the wine lists are labels ranging from Alsace's Valentin Zusslin and Burgundy's Eleonore Moreau, to South Africa's Jumpin Juice and Australia's Carousal. There's no food on the menu, and for good reason: the Commons is filled to the brim with excellent eateries, offering everything from Taiwanese hotpot to lobster rolls and dim sums. There's also another outpost in Baan Turtle, Soi Suanplu.

@cloudwinebottleshop TEL +66 98 814 8997

127 KANGKAO WINE CLUB

469 Prasumen Rd, Bangkok 10200, Thailand

TO VISIT BEFORE YOU DIE BECAUSE

Specialising in natural wines, this atmospheric, chilled-out bar is hard to find and hard to leave

Like many of Bangkok's best finds, this tiny wine bar is slightly hidden away. First enter the third-floor Ku Bar, then once inside, go back down to the second floor for Kangkao. Both bars are the creations of Elaine Sun, who moved from New York to Bangkok, where she so missed drinking natural wines that she decided to take matters into her own hands. Opened in 2018, Kangkao was the first and only natural wine bar in the capital. 'At the time it was very new to Thai customers so it was hard but exciting to introduce the concept and taste of these wines to our guests,' says Elaine, whose unofficial motto is 'no somms, no chefs, no bullshit'. On her wine list are perennial favourites such as skin-contact whites from Matassa (Roussillon), juicy reds from Clos du Tue-Boeuf (a family-run operation in the Loire) and tiny-batch experimental cuvees from Momento Mori (Australia). Snacks include braised lotus stems and pickled chilli pepper with cold cuts from Larder BKK.

@kang.kao TEL +66 2 067 6731

128 RIEDEL WINE BAR & CELLAR

Gaysorn Village 2nd floor, 999 Phloenchit Rd, Lumphini, Bangkok 10330, Thailand

TO VISIT BEFORE YOU DIE BECAUSE

This high-spec, high-tech bar celebrates the power of Riedel's stemware and offers wine on tap

The starting point for this bar and restaurant in the upmarket Gaysorn Village shopping mall is not the wine, but the glass it goes into. Not any glass, though: we're talking about Riedel Crystal stemware here, also known as 'the loudspeaker of wine'. No point having a loudspeaker if you've nothing to say, but thankfully there's plenty to talk about here, with an extensive wine list comprising over 250 labels with an emphasis on the artisanal and authentic. These include 40 wines available on tap, using the state-of-the-art Wine Emotion dispensing and preservation system. At the push of a button wines can be enjoyed in three different portions: tasting, half-glass and full glass, poured correctly, at the perfect temperature, into the perfect Riedel glass. There's a great programme of events, including Meet the Makers Tapas and Wine Flight evenings with guests such as Germany's Dr Loosen. An elaborate menu features dishes such as truffle soup and conch ceviche.

@riedel.bkk

TEL +66 2 656 1133

129 TERROIRS BY LQV

3rd floor, 1 Lyndhurst Terrace, Central, Hong Kong

TO VISIT
BEFORE YOU DIE
BECAUSE

The best of French wines and products have been teleported to this elegant brasserie in central Hong Kong

LQV first opened its doors as a wine shop and deli in Paris in 2010, then launched various bars and food shops in Hong Kong. The latest venue to offer a slice of France's gastronomy and savoir-faire in the skyscraper city is Terroirs, which opened in 2022 on Lyndhurst Terrace. Spread across two balconies, a bar and a dining area, it is a welcoming space designed by LC Studio using wood, stone and terracotta. The food menu features French classics such as a *croque-monsieur* with truffle ham, *pâté en croute* and lemon tart, with a helpful map showing where the ingredients come from. The wine list is all about France with every single region represented, from Alsace to Corsica (although there are also a few bottles from Switzerland's Wallis and Germany's Baden and Moselle). There are more than 2,000 wine references, which the team says equates to a 'Michelin-starred wine list without the Michelin prices or requisite ceremony.'

terroirsbylqv.com TEL +852 2550 0345

130 COUPE DE VIN

First Floor, 180 Jalan Tun HS Lee, Kuala Lumpur City centre, 50000 Kuala Lumpur, Malaysia

TO VISIT BEFORE YOU DIE BECAUSE

A uniquely designed spot to enjoy wine by the glass in the true melting pot that is central Kuala Lumpur

Opened in 2022 in Kuala Lumpur's Chinatown, this wine bar is perched on the first floor of a small building, just above the fancy pâtisserie Flaon, and offers a truly original haven from the bustling crowds heading to the nearby Central Market. Named after the French for 'glass of wine' and inspired by its shape, it is a free-flowing space full of curvy features, from round stools and sinuous seating to organic tabletops and cave-like openings. Even the neon logo is twisty and full of movement. For such a small space, it also offers great views of its surroundings, thanks to a large glass ceiling and wall: on one side is the Merdeka 118 skyscraper (the second tallest structure in the world), and on the other side the colourful Sri Mahamariamman Temple. Among its selection of wines by the glass you will find a 'beautifully rich, lush and full-flavoured' 30 Mile Shiraz 2017 from Australia, a Valpolicella Ripasso Classico Superiore 'with ripe red cherry and plum flavours', and a Matarromera Reserva 2017 with 'a subtle mineral nuance typical of the limestone soils where it is born'.

@coupedevin_180

131 VETRO & ENOTECA

The Oberoi, Mumbai, Nariman Point, Mumbai, Maharashtra 400021, India

TO VISIT BEFORE YOU DIE BECAUSE

Celebrate the global influence of Italy's food and wine culture at this five-star joint on Mumbai's seafront

Wine bars are slowly popping up in India's big cities, but oenophiles can still count on one hand places like Vetro & Enoteca in the five-star Oberoi Hotel on Marine Drive. One of the city's few dedicated wine libraries, it holds 1,200 bottles of the finest wines, including one of the largest offerings of Italian wines in the country. It was designed as a preamble to the delicious Italian fare at Vetro, with guests encouraged to come early for dinner in order to enjoy the glass-enclosed wine library. Surrounded by floor-to-ceiling displays of wine, you can sit at a special table for wine and cheese tasting, where you sample a selection of three white and three red wines before deciding on the perfect bottle to accompany your meal. Highlights include Louis Roederer Cristal and Dom Pérignon brut champagnes, as well as white wines such as a 2009 Château Guiraud, 1er Grand Cru Classé, Sauternes, and reds ranging from a 2003 Château Mouton Rothschild to a 2019 Tenuta San Guido, Sassicaia, Bolgheri. Look out for special wine and food pairing events.

oberoihotels.com/hotels-in-mumbai/restaurants/vetro-and-enoteca

TEL +91 22 6632 6215

132 LA COPA OSCURA

No. 69, Lane 39, Section 1, Shipai Rd,
Beitou, Taipei City 112, Taiwan

TO VISIT
BEFORE YOU DIE
BECAUSE

A perfect blend of Asian minimalism and Spanish warmth, this Taipei bar specialises in Spanish wines

Located in north Taipei, La Copa Oscura is a zen-like space with deep terracotta walls, and specialises in wines by the glass, including organic, biodynamic, natural and amphora wines. It was founded by young sommelier Wang Yiting, a blind-tasting champion who graduated with a tri-country master's degree in wine management that involved stints in Angers (France), Bolonia (Italy) and Valencia (Spain). It was during the last that she discovered a passion for Spanish wines. 'I have so many favourite wines, but if I had to choose one it would be Salanques from the Mas Doix winery in Tarragona,' says Wang. 'Not only for its flavour and taste, but because that's my starting point of Spanish wines–powerful, elegant and deep, all at once.' From Bizkaiko Txakolina to Terra Alta, all Spanish regions are represented here (plus wines by Montenegro's Lipovac winery), with full notes and explanations about each winery. There is also a selection of Mediterranean-inspired dishes and tapas, drinks such as Vichy Catalan sparkling water, as well as special courses and tastings, focusing on themes such as the Marselan grape variety.

lacopaoscura.com

TEL +886 2 2823 0234

COPA OSCURA

探杯子
WINE
OLIVE OIL
COSMETICS

133 BAR 81

Lotte World Tower, Signiel Seoul 81F, 300 Olympic-ro, Songpa-gu, Seoul, South Korea

TO VISIT BEFORE YOU DIE BECAUSE

It's the highest champagne bar in the world, with dizzying views and a head-spinning selection of bubblies

Dominating the Seoul Cityscape is the Lotte World Tower, a gently tapering, supertall skyscraper that houses the luxury Signiel Hotel on its 76th-101st floors. And on the 81st floor is this upscale champagne bar, boasting the largest champagne collection in South Korea. Settle down and enjoy the magnificent views and an extensive list of unique Recoltant Manipulant champagnes selected by the award-winning sommelier, Yang Dae-hoon (Lucas Yang). There are slick walls featuring stones imported from the Champagne region; glitzy ceiling installations recalling the sparkling drink; and over 80 different types of champagne (including natural ones). The best-selling champagne is the Champagne Victoire Prestige Brut, which can be enjoyed only at Bar 81 in Korea. Pairing Champagne with food is a pleasure here, thanks to the dishes specially developed by Michelin-starred chef Yannick Alléno. And once you get back down to earth, make sure to check out the rest of Seoul's blossoming wine scene, including bars such as Clos de Young, Dogokokk and Geumnam Vin.

lottehotel.com/seoul-signiel/en/dining/bar-81.html

TEL +82 2 3213 1281

134 PUDAO WINES

376 Wukang Rd, Xu Hui Qu, Shang Hai Shi, China, 200031

TO VISIT BEFORE YOU DIE BECAUSE

This Shanghai stalwart offers great wines by the glass in a lovely courtyard setting

The second outpost of wine distributor Summergate's well-respected Pudao Wines is located in Shanghai's Shankang Li, an area of Jing'an, brimming with restaurants and delis. Its shop is stocked with around 1,200 bottles from around the world, white its tasting room comes with an imposing floor-to-ceiling wine fridge. Its best asset is the bar: not only can you enjoy people watching, it also offers the opportunity to sample over 30 vintages by the glasses, including Chinese wines such as Ningxia's Silver Heights. If the weather is nice, crowds often spill out onto the busy courtyard, and they've no reason to leave, as they are welcome to take their pick from the neighbouring food joints to accompany their glass of wine. Pudao Wines' original location, on Ferguson Lane in the French Concession, is also well worth a visit, with an equally interesting selection of wines and a lovely rooftop terrace from which to enjoy them.

pudaowines.com

TEL +86 21 6090 7075

135 SOIF

Room 105, 550 Wuding Road, Shanghai, China

TO VISIT BEFORE YOU DIE BECAUSE

One of Shanghai's leading natural wine bars, Soif also offers great food in a lovely contemporary setting

Focusing on 'no added nonsense' natural wines, this neighbourhood bar in Shanghai's Jing'an District was opened in 2019 by Montrealer François Séguin-Letendre and his local partners. Since then, they have quickly established themselves as pioneers of the natural wine bar movement in China, leading to a series of signature events, pop-ups and partnerships. Soif means 'thirst' in French, and here you can definitely have your fill, with a by the glass selection that offers guests the opportunity to discover new wines from around the world, from France's Laurent Saillard to the Czech Republic's Milan Nestarec. To complement the wine cellar is a menu of small plates created by chef Freddy Raoult, who finds inspiration in his native France, but also in Finland, where he worked for a decade. Popular dishes include house-made charcuterie (such as duck breast prosciutto, pig's head roulade or salami made of squid ink and pork), Korean-style beef tartare and torched sardine on a gazpacho-dipped toast.

@soifshanghai

TEL +86 199 2133 9217

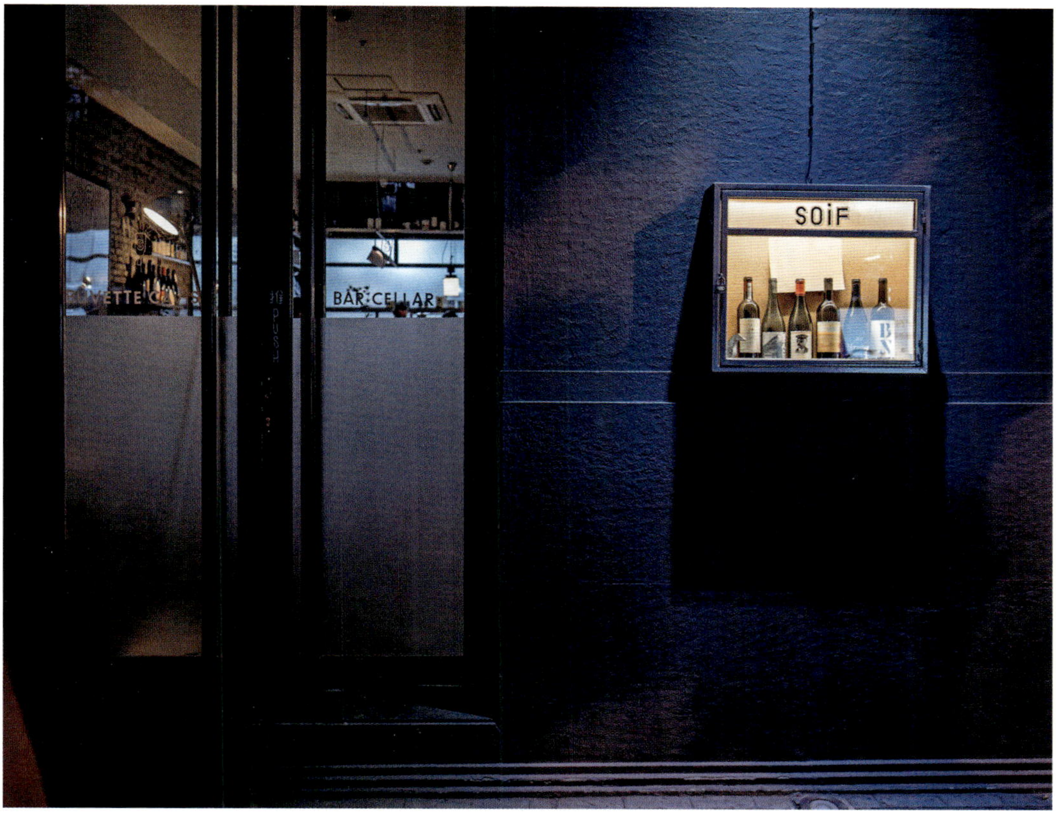
SOïF
BAR CELLAR
PUSH

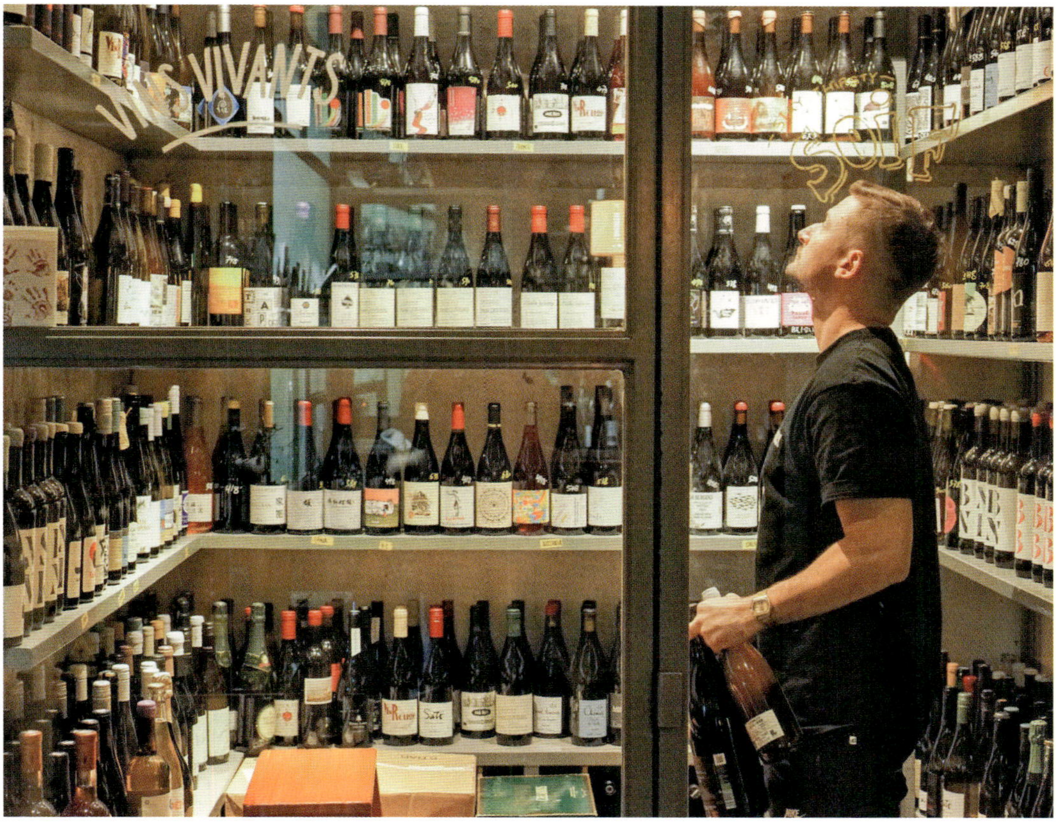
VIVANTS

136 PARK90

Conrad Orchard Road, 1 Cuscaden Rd, Singapore 249715

TO VISIT
BEFORE YOU DIE
BECAUSE

A must for Singapore's wine lovers, this hotel bar offers hundreds of references, including some sought-after Burgundies

Part of wine platform Wine Portal's portfolio, this classy fine-wine bar is located in the newly refurbished five-star Conrad Hotel, near Singapore's bustling Orchard Road. It is named after the Robert Parker Wine Advocate's rating system created by Robert Parker in 1978, with most of the wines served at Park90 rated RP90 points and above. The menu features more than 800 labels, including hard-to-get Burgundy domains, and a complementary menu of sharing plates from both the award-winning Basilico and the Michelin-starred Summer Palace (whose deep-fried frog legs with Chinese five spice are definitely worth a try). It's the only place in Singapore where you can drink Domaine de la Romanée-Conti and Pétrus by the glass. Head sommelier Mason Ng can guide you through the selection, which also includes bottles from the family-run Domaine Dujac, organic Maison Jean Fournier and biodynamic producer Champagne Marguet. Park90 also has an outpost, Tenuta by Park90, at the InterContinental, which focuses on Italian wines.

park90.com TEL +65 6733 8888

137 RVLT

38 Carpenter Street, #01-01, Singapore 059917

TO VISIT BEFORE YOU DIE BECAUSE

Upbeat and unpretentious, this cool bar has a cult following thanks to its excellent wine selection and food

This 'ridiculously fun winebar' near Clarke Quay was founded in 2017 by an energetic duo of sommeliers, Alvin Gho and Ian Lim, who like to share their personal favourites and new discoveries with their guests. 'Our aim is to showcase wines that are off the beaten track, and vignerons, working with minimal intervention made with clean grapes,' says Lim. 'Our wines are always changing, so we don't have a physical wine list, but currently we are really excited about grower champagnes.' To make it onto RVLT's iconic wine wall, bottles have to be juicy and smashable; the latest picks include a bottle of Zibbibo amber wine by Sicily's Marco de Bartoli, and Fontaine des Grives Merlots from south-west France. The food, by chef Sunny Leong, is also fun and fresh: everything is made in house and they even bake their own bread daily (it's served with seaweed and Arbequina olive oil). Favourites include chicken nuggets with homemade sriracha, beef tartare with sago dashi crackers, hand-cut pasta with confit lobster tail, and calamansi citrus tart.

winervlt.sg

TEL +65 6909 5709

THANK YOU
FOR YOUR S.G.
CONTRIBUTIONS!

WINE
INGUEVARA
hasta el terroir siempre

138 GOÛT DE JAUNE

2-chome-19-4 Akasaka, Minato City, Tokyo 107-0052, Japan

TO VISIT BEFORE YOU DIE BECAUSE

'The holy land of Jura wine lovers', this Tokyo bar offers thousands of bottles from the French wine region

This tiny, 13-seat underground bar in Tokyo's Akasaka is completely and uniquely dedicated to celebrating the delicious wines of one very specific département of France, Jura. This mountainous area near the border with Switzerland is primarily known for its *vin jaune*, a wine made from late-harvest Savagnin grapes matured in a barrel under a film of yeast, and similar in taste to dry Fino sherry. The little-known eastern department certainly deserves the focus, as it is also home to the sweet *vin de paille*; Morbier, Comté and Mont d'Or cheeses; tasty sausages and dishes such as *coq au vin jaune*, all of which you can sample here. Forget the hustle and bustle of Tokyo and settle down at the bar with a cheese platter and a glass of Château-Chalon for a first-class ticket to a French gourmet experience. There's also some freshly cooked Chinese fare, which pairs perfectly with the wine's nutty, umami notes.

goutdejaune.com TEL +81 3 5545 5205

139 WINESHOP FLOW

Clover Building B1F, 2 Chome-28-3, Nishihara, Shibuya City, Tokyo 151-0066, Japan

TO VISIT BEFORE YOU DIE BECAUSE

One of Shibuya's coolest bars and wine shops, this minimalist place offers great wines and great beats

Near Hatagaya Station in Shibuya, on a typical Tokyo lane with mismatched townhouses and dangling wires, you will find this great little wine cellar and bar. Clad in stripes of blond timber, it sells only natural wine, craft beer and a few snacks and platters (with some daily specials delivered by local friends and restaurateurs, including Kasiki ice creams). Behind the bar you will find owner Kenmitsu Fukagawa, also known as Kenkou, who is also a musician (which explains the great sound system and beats). Every day he selects three white wines, three reds, one *pét nat* and one rosé by the glass. A round portal leads to the cellar itself, from which you can select a bottle to take home or enjoy on the spot with a corkage fee. Sit at one of the long communal tables to sample bottles such as the Japanese Michinoku, or the Cuvée Tohoku 2018 by France's Pierre-Olivier Bonhomme. There's also lots of special events, from food and wine pairing to winemaker visits.

@wineshop_flow

140 APÉRO

280 Karangahape Rd, Auckland 1010, New Zealand

TO VISIT BEFORE YOU DIE BECAUSE

This friendly family business, set in the heart of Auckland's creative hub, is run with passion and care

Named after the favourite pastime in France (snacks and drinks with friends before a meal), Apéro is a warm, welcoming place with exposed brick walls and Tolix metal stools, in a former tattoo parlour on Karangahape Road. It's the passion project of partners Leslie Hottiaux and Ismo (Mo) Koski. Leslie, who hails from Toulouse, looks after the kitchen, where she produces French classics such as terrines, *pâtés en croute* and charcuterie. Her signature dish is homemade sausage, sold by the quarter, the half or full metre (you can never have too much it seems!), with roast cauliflower a close second. Mo, whose family is originally from Finland, manages front of house and picks the wines to create an eclectic selection; 'There are no rules to the list, other than it must be delicious.' Regular visits to small winemakers throughout New Zealand include local finds such as Saorsa Wines, small-production artisan wines made from the finest plots in Hawke's Bay.

apero.co.nz

TEL +64 9 373 4778

141 SCOTCH WINE BAR

24-26 Maxwell Rd, Blenheim Central, Blenheim 7201, New Zealand

TO VISIT BEFORE YOU DIE BECAUSE

At the heart of New Zealand's wine industry, this bar offers fun blind-tasting nights and winemaker-led events

Located in Marlborough, a region of South Island home to some of the country's finest winemakers, Blenheim is known as the gateway to the wineries of the Wairau Valley to the west. But before you head out to one of the 30 surrounding vineyards, we suggest a pitstop at Scotch, Jacob Anderson's wine bar and bottle shop, which is loved by visiting oenophiles and local winemakers alike. 'We have an extensive wine list that features over 300 wines from around the globe, focusing on smaller producers with organic and biodynamic principles and certifications,' says Anderson, a Marlborough native. Events include blind-tasting nights and winemaker-led or region-focused tastings, while the weekly changing selection of wines by the glass features the likes of local producers Greywacke, Dog Point and Fromm. Also not to be missed is the award-winning food menu, featuring dishes such as butterfish, kimchi and green tea broth, and almond tart with fermented honeycomb and blueberries.

scotchbar.co.nz TEL +64 3 579 1176

142 LUCINDA

123 Collins St, Hobart TAS 7000, Australia

TO VISIT
BEFORE YOU DIE
BECAUSE

Set up by one of Tasmania's rising stars, this small wine bar, focusing on natural wines, is the new place to be

Chef Kobi Ruzicka had always dreamed of opening his own bar, so when a space came up just next to his destination restaurant, Dier Makr in central Hobart, he of course snapped it up and set up Lucinda. Focusing on natural wines, with a freewheeling menu and great music, the bar has become as well known as its neighbour. 'Our list varies in size but sometimes has as many as 700 natural wines, from Australia to France, South Africa and Hungary, even wines from Japan such as Miyagi and Yamagata,' says Ruzicka, who is originally from Melbourne. 'Our food offering is based on Tasmanian organic or wild caught produce, starting with oysters. It could be as simple as some line-caught fish served raw with pickled peppers and fried curry leaf, or zucchini flowers stuffed with rock lobster.' Grab a seat on the terrace and enjoy the award-winning wine list featuring Australia's Brave New Wine, Momento Mori, Limus Wines and the beautifully named Place of Changing Winds.

lucindawine.com

TEL

143 OLD PALM LIQUOR

133B Lygon St, Brunswick East VIC 3057, Australia

TO VISIT BEFORE YOU DIE BECAUSE

A great neighbourhood bar where you can sample South African-inspired food and a painstakingly assembled wine list

This is the type of place you dream of stumbling upon when visiting a new city. On its windows are signs reading 'Beer', 'Wine' and 'Meals', but there's no mention of the lovely space inside—a stylish bar and spacious dining room, lit by skylights and full of greenery. Opened in 2019, it is the second venture of Almay Jordaan and Simon Denman (their first is Neighbourhood Wine) and centres around a South African grill, or *braai*. 'The *braai* is inspired by how we cook at home, and reflects the experiences and flavours Almay grew up with, an example being the Cape Malay spices that show up on grilled fish or oysters,' explains Simon, who himself is in charge of the décor and the wine list, which has been a decade in the making. It includes 'rare wines from some of the world's great artisanal wine producers and leans heavily on the domestic lo-fi wine scene,' as well as sparkling wines from around the world (including Chile, Japan and Switzerland) and local labels such as Jamsheed Wines, Tidy Town and Dirty Black Denim.

oldpalmliquor.com TEL +61 3 9380 2132

144 CITY WINE SHOP

159 Spring St, Melbourne VIC 3000, Australia

TO VISIT BEFORE YOU DIE BECAUSE

A Melbourne classic beloved by both theatregoers and wine lovers, with a showstopping range of wines by the glass

When owners Josh Brisbane and Con Christopoulos opened the doors of the City Wine Shop in 2004, it was one of the first spaces of its kind in Melbourne. Inspired by the Italian *enoteca*, it is both a shop and bar, with blackboard menus, green tiled walls and tables spilling out onto the street. Food comes from sibling restaurant and neighbour The European, with a particular favourite being the chicken schnitzel served with handmade Italian coleslaw, while bar snacks include both humble *pan con tomate*, and oysters and Yarra Valley caviar. There's a huge range of wines by the glass, which rotate week to week and showcase some of the world's best wine producers. Bottlewise, you could pick the likes of House of Arras 'Brut Elite Cuvée' sparkling from Tasmania, Rockford Eden Valley Riesling, or a Fraser Gallop Parterre Chardonnay from Margaret River. Also represented are lots of Victoria winegrowers, such as Bass Philip Estate, Fighting Gully and Schmölzer & Brown.

citywineshop.net.au

TEL +61 3 9654 6657

PRINTERS
WINE SHOP
N WINES 
MARGARET RIVER
FRANKLAND ESTATE
S.C. PANNELL
WINEMAKER
MOUN
VINI

wine shop
City Wine Shop
Bottle Shop Open Late
Seven Days
Victorian, Australian & European Wine Selection
Extensive range of Champagne and Malt Whisky
Local and Imported Lagers and Ales
Drink-in or Takeaway
Breakfast Menu
All Day Meals
Wine Food & Cheese
Monthly Wine Tastings
Dinners and Events
Local Interstate & Overseas Wine Delivery
Wine Food Specials
Main Specials
Soup: Minestrone
Fish: Grilled Dory, Smoked Chats, Pepperonata
Braised Veal Shanks
Pearl Barley, Root Vegetables and a Spinach & Herb Crumb
Menu
Desserts

159
wine shop
CITY WINE SHOP
WWW.CITYWINESHOP.NET.AU
Bottle Shop–
Open Seven Days
VICTORIAN, AUSTRALIAN
& European Wine SELECTION
Extensive Range of
CHAMPAGNE AND
MALT WHISKY–
LOCAL AND IMPORTED
Lagers AND Ales
DRINK-IN OR TAKEAWAY
Breakfast Menu
ALL DAY MEALS from 12pm
WINE FOOD & CHEESE
Monthly Wine tastings
Dinners and events
LOCAL, INTERSTATE &
OVERSEAS DELIVERY

145 VINOTTO PERTH

Lot 2/137 Claremont Cres, Swanbourne WA 6010, Australia

TO VISIT BEFORE YOU DIE BECAUSE

This popular local hangout is a friendly place to sample Aussie favourites in Western Australia

When it opened in 2022, this long-awaited little wine bar in Perth's Swanbourne district filled up in under an hour, with a queue snaking round the block for the rest of the evening. Locals had had a glimpse of its handsome terrazzo counter, open kitchen and bottle-lined shelves, and wanted a piece of the action. It wasn't a flash in the pan: Vinotto is still thriving today, thanks to the excellent work of chef Justin Wong and sommelier/manager Caitlin Johnston. You could do much worse than settling in at the back by a window overlooking the courtyard garden, and sampling Aussie favourites such as Jauma Wines (an organically farmed vineyard in the Adelaide Hills), Blind Corner (a family-owned, certified organic and biodynamic vineyard and winery in Western Australia) and MDI Wines (Pinot Grigio and Sangiovese from the Murray Darling, with a punk edge). To accompany the wine, you can tuck into a plate of creamy burrata, crispy fried chicken with pickles and bulldog mayo or scallops with *sauce gribiche*.

vinotto.com.au

146 THE WINE LIBRARY

18 Oxford St, Woollahra NSW 2025, Australia

TO VISIT
BEFORE YOU DIE
BECAUSE

Run by a dedicated oenophile, this wine bar is the place to taste rare wines and cult vintages

One of Sydney's original wine bars, The Wine Library is tucked away at the top of Oxford Street in Woollahra, in Sydney's Eastern suburbs. Its head sommelier and owner, Tim Perlstone, has won a multitude of awards and scholarships, including the Ruinart Challenge and the Lorenzo Galli, to name a few. 'Our list focuses on the eclectic with a lean towards natural wine including orange, skin contact, organic and biodynamic wine,' he says. 'However, there are wines for all tastes and preferences. Our list includes rare, cult and old vintage wines averaging 800 wines by the bottle and 65 by the glass.' Pick and mix from a Provençal Clos Cibonne Tibourenne or a Sicilian Nerocapitano Frappato, or stay local with a cult 'Texture Like Sun Field Red Sector Eight' 2022 by Ochota Barrels, Adelaide Hills, or Jilly Wine Co's Banana Girl skin contact wine from the Central Tablelands. Chef Matheus Costa dishes plates small and large, including mouth-watering Gruyère croquettes served with aioli, while events include masterclasses and winemaker dinners.

wine-library.com.au TEL +61 2 9368 7484

THE ENGLISH WHISKY Co.
TALISKER
LAPHROAIG
Ardbeg
GLENMORANGIE
TEMPLETON RYE
JAMESON
Maker's Mark
FOUR PILLARS
ARCHIE ROSE
BEEFEATER
MADEIRA
43

WINE LIBRARY
Sydney Australia
EST. 2010
MODA
Still
MODA
Sparkling

147 VINI DIVINI

G2A/60 Carrington St, Sydney NSW 2000, Australia

TO VISIT
BEFORE YOU DIE
BECAUSE

It's a stylish bar with a great selection of wines by the glass, both from Australia and some of the world's oldest winegrowing regions

This homely Mediterranean-inspired wine bar is the brainchild of Philippe Gilbert, whose globetrotting family ran the first Italian delis and ice cream carts in Belgium between the world wars. After stints in New York, France and Greece, Gilbert has settled down in Sydney with his Australian wife and young family. Just like his grandmother used to bring joy and good food to people in dark times, Gilbert aims to bring people together 'to laugh, pour wine, break bread and share stories or ideas' around Vini Divini's large central bar. On the menu you'll find small plates of marinated artichokes and various salami and cheese selections, while the wine by-the-glass selection includes a NV Ca' di Alte Prosecco, a 2021 Gilbert Blanc Pinot Gris orange wine from New South Wales and a 2019 Tetramythos Retsina Amphora Roditis from the Peloponnese in Greece. Wine flights have intriguing names such as Ancient Greek and Birthplace Wines (from Georgia and Turkey), and there are also three different types of non-alcoholic wine.

vinidivini.com.au

TEL +61 477 033 811

BOLLA

RIKARD

148 PASKI VINERIA POPOLARE

239 Oxford Street, Darlinghurst NSW 2010, Australia

TO VISIT BEFORE YOU DIE BECAUSE

This bustling wine bar offers a tempting choice of artisan-made Italian wines and great small plates

Italian wine importers Giorgio De Maria and Mattia Dicati opened this small restaurant and wine bar in Sydney's cosmopolitan Darlinghurst with chef Enrico Tomelleri in 2021. Head downstairs for the bar, which features illuminated shelving displaying the full 400-bottle range of artisanal Italian wine on offer, including bottles from the likes of Cantina Giardino, Le Coste and Pacina. Here, along with a glass of Italian Valli Unite or French Talweg, you can enjoy Tomelleri's small plates—antispasti such as focaccia and marinated aubergine, casarecce pasta with prawn arrabiata or baked cheesecake. Upstairs is the trattoria, with rare and special wines on the menu and heartier pairings such as short ribs and Barolo, and regional Italian specialties such as *cjarsons*, a filled pasta from Friuli stuffed with potato, chard and apples. Decorated with a modern take on Leonardo da Vinci's *Last Supper* by Turin-based artist Gianluca Cannizzo, the space is used for tastings on Wednesday nights.

paski.com.au

149 NOBLE ROT

6 Swan Lane, Te Aro, Wellington 6011, New Zealand

TO VISIT BEFORE YOU DIE BECAUSE

This Wellington institution is the place to enjoy fine wines and good food in a unique historic setting

Housed in a 100-year-old building full of character and rustic charm, this cosy European-inspired wine bar and restaurant first opened its doors in 2016. Its vast wine list comprises almost 1,000 references from premium wineries around New Zealand and the world, plus nearly 100 wines available by the glass. The red Burgundy section is substantial and covers the biggest range of producers and vintages, while the glass-pour selection changes frequently and is split between two sections, Sommelier and Coravin, to present different levels of wine complexity and calibre. Here, you can sit under one of the four bespoke two-tier chandeliers made by a local company using bottles enjoyed at Noble Rot, and snack on the ever-popular chicken liver parfait. Or go for one of the Noble Selection degustation menus, with expertly matched wines chosen by the award-winning sommelier team—including Jessica Wood and co-owner Maciej Zimny—and designed to take the customers on a wine journey around the world.

noblerot.co.nz TEL +64 4 385 6671

150 THE PUFFIN

60 Ghuznee St, Te Aro, Wellington 6011, New Zealand

TO VISIT
BEFORE YOU DIE
BECAUSE

This deftly decorated wine bar has an incredible wine list and a friendly and knowledgeable team

Located in the former Cadbury Brothers building, this bar specialising in organic and low-intervention wines is accessed through a blink-and-you'll-miss-it atmospheric tiled entrance hall. Once inside, you can choose between three different spaces: a dramatically lit main bar with exposed brick walls and centrepiece chandelier, a cosy parlour lounge or the bright conservatory. 'We have a list of by-the-glass options that changes weekly and a bottle list of about 200 bottles that could be considered more of a deep dive into the wines we offer,' says the friendly, seven-strong team. 'We select wines from New Zealand and all over the world—Australia, France, Spain, Italy, South Africa, Portugal and beyond.' Their aim is to give guests an exceptional experience, which means 'they can talk about the wine as much or as little as they want to'. Local labels include the organic Millton Vineyards and Halcyon Wines, as well as artisanal beers, while snacks include garlic bread with bone broth butter or crudités and aioli.

puffinwinebar.com TEL +64 04 830 0996

About the author

> Jurgen Lijcops is an excellent taster who not only has a near-encyclopedic knowledge of drinks but also is a naturally gifted host and entertainer.
> — Peter Goossens, Hof van Cleve

Jurgen Lijcops studied at the Burgundy Wine School in Beaune and then went to work as an assistant sommelier at the renowned Scholteshof restaurant. After becoming head sommelier at the Scholteshof, Lijcops moved to the two-star Slagmolen restaurant in Opglabbeek. Next, he was promoted to maître sommelier at the three-star Bruneau restaurant in Brussels. He subsequently worked as manager of the ambitious Withof project at the castle of Brasschaat. In 2009 he opened the Glorious on Antwerp's Zuid. It immediately became one of the city's leading restaurants, even gaining a Michelin star. In 2016 he set up Bar Burbure, which was proclaimed 'Best Bar Concept' that very same year. Lijcops has twice been named best sommelier in Belgium and best host in Belgium by Gault-Millau. Constantly striving to update his knowledge of drinks, he travels the world, discovering the most exquisite bars in which to sit back and sip the best cocktails and spirits.

About Bar Burbure

> Jurgen Lijcops is doing a great deal for the Belgian bar scene with Bar Burbure, establishing a high-end cocktail bar that can compete with those in London, Milan and New York! A must-visit when in Belgium!
> — Ran van Ongevalle, winner of the Global Bacardi Legacy competition

> True class and style with the finest spirit selection and clever cocktails! Very well done!
> — Martin Hudak, the Savoy's American Bar, London

> I had a wonderful time at Bar Burbure; the details of both the venue and the service make for a destination drinking experience, not only in Belgium but surely in Europe!
> — Remy Savage, head bartender, Artesian, London

Amid gorgeous green tiles and modern copper fixtures, patrons can enjoy the finest of cocktails in a cosy, well-appointed corner bar in Antwerp's museum district. With a full bar, including premium-label liquors, liqueurs, cognacs and whiskys, plus its own trademark Forest line of specialty spirits, **Bar Burbure** offers you an array of delicious libations. The carefully curated wine list changes seasonally. Beer aficionados will be delighted to discover the Westvleteren Trappist range, plus the renowned Czech-crafted Pilsner Urquell on tap.Bar Burbure has a fine selection of Spanish sherries from Bodegas Tradición, and cigars are available for enjoying outside on the terrace. Fashionable Milan, quaint London and cosmopolitan Manhattan all blend together in Bar Burbure, making it Antwerp's epicentre for relaxing and unwinding in quiet sophistication.

Index 150 Winebars

© Photos

p.10 Franck Laine / p.11 Franck Laine / p.12 13C bar in the back / p.13 L'appartement / p.16 The Bar at Nile Plaza / p.17 Culture / p. 18 Leo's / p. 19 Publik Wine Bar / p.20 Jumeirah Hotels & Resorts / p.21 Cave Dubai / pp. 22-23 Cave Dubai / p. 24 Grapeskin / p.25 Grapeskin / p.26 Devin Lester / p.27 Rocker Media / p.28 Marcos De Rada / p.29 Lukas Stander / p.30 Bartinney Wine & Champagne Bar / p.31 The Wine Glass Stellenbosch / p.32 Haim Yosef / p.33 Hila Ramati Harel / p.34 Cava Wine / p.35 Jon Pack / p.36 Máximo Pereyra Iraola / p.37 Solera almacén de vinos y tapas / p.38 Hay pan / p.39 Cordial & Foodfreak / p.40 David Peng / p.41 Jordana Hazel / pp. 42-43 Jakob Layman / p.44 Bar Bandini / p.45 Aline Valdes / pp. 46 – 47 Wine Bar by Concours Mondial de Bruxelles / p.48 Local 1 / p.49 Vigneron / p.50 Elemento / p.51 MRDK / p.52 MRDK / p.53 MRDK / p.54 Bounty Hunter / p.55 Francesco Tonelli / pp. 56 – 57 Francesco Tonelli / p.58 Collin Hughes / p.59 Air's Champagne Parlor / p.60 Liz Clayman / p.61 Erik Castro / p.62 Neal Santos / p.63 Adam Milliron / p.64 Charl Marl / p.65 The Winehouse / p.66 Grace Sager / p.67 Buddy / pp. 68 – 69 Albert Law / p. 70 Denise Portugueiz / p.71 Katherine Hidalgo / p.72 Enoteca Saint Vinsaint / p.73 Danielle Adams / p.74 Bar Gobo / p.75 Scott Suchman / pp.76 – 77 Scott Suchman / p.78 Studio BVD / p.79 Bubbles & Wines / p.80 Axelle Verhoustraeten / p.81 Axelle Verhoustraeten / p.82 Cava Vegera / p.83 Heteroclito / p.84 Alex Antoniadis / p.85 Alex Antoniadis / p.86 Monika Frias / p.87 Monika Frias / p.88 Roberta Sant'Anna / p.89 Bobbi Shewchuk / p.90 Freundschaft / p.91 Ora / p.92 Ora / p.93 Ora / p.94 Wim Jansen / p.95 (top) Robert Rieger / p.95 (bottom) Wim Jansen / p.96 Vineria Favalli / p.97 R. Savry / pp.98 – 99 G. Bonnaud / p.100 Ann-Sophie Deldycke / p.101 Bar du Canal / p.102 eating.be / p.103 Giuseppe Liverino / p.104 Bar'vin / p.105 Bar'vin / p.106 Al Higgins / p.107 Al Higgins / p.108 Le Di-Vin / p.109 Die Weinbank Wirtshaus / pp.110 - 111 Die Weinbank Wirtshaus / p.112 Chez Bacchus / p.113 Jean-Paul Bastian / p.114 Muru's Winebar / p.115 Apotek /p.116 Vigneron Wine House / p.117 Vigneron Wine House / p.118 Czarna Owca Wine Bar / p.119 Gabriela Weil / p.120 Paulo Fernando / p.121 Movia / p.122 Julie Limont / p.123 Julie Limont / p.124 Harry East / p.125 Paul Marc Mitchell / pp. 126 – 127 Chio Photography / p.128 Noble Rot Wine Bar & Restaurant/ p.129 Noble Rot Wine Bar & Restaurant / pp.130 – 131 Noble Rot Wine Bar & Restaurant / p.132 James Hines / p.133 Searcy's Champagne Bar / p.134 Nosch / p.135 La Cave Café Terroir / p.136 De Vinos / p.137 Berria / pp.138 – 139 Berria / p.140 Vinology / p.141 Vinology / p.142 Voila Vé / p.143 Ciz Cantina e cucina / p.144 Juliette Elodie Bellavita / p.145 Enoteca Internazionale / p.146 Markus Bassler / p.147 Mina Taaje / p.148 Nektar / p.149 Vin Bjørvika / pp. 150 – 151 Vin Bjørvika / p.152 Ferramenta / p.153 Anthony Perez / p.154 Avant Comptoir de la Mer / p.155 TGP / p.156 Pierre Renauld / p.157 Pierre Renauld / p.158 Legrand Filles & Fils / p.159 Legrand Filles & Fils / p.160 Franck Joyeux / p.161 Yann Deret / pp. 162-163 Yann Deret / p.164 Capela Incomum / p.165 Capela Incomum / p.166 Vinoteka Sodček / p. 167 Planda Architecte / p.168 D'Emblée Film / p.169 Il Piccolo / pp.170 – 171 Il Piccolo / p.172 Fou / p.173 Ganbara / p.174 Leon Sinowenka / p.175 Julia Heydkamp / pp.176-177 Julia Heydkamp / p.178 Combo / p.179 Alsace à Boire / p.180 Alsace à Boire / p.181 Alsace à Boire / p.182 Die Mosel / p.183 Die Mosel / pp.184 – 185 Die Mosel / p.186 Roosa Karhu / p.187 Athanasios Aléxo / p.188 Karuna Clayton / p.189 Mast / pp.190 – 191 Christian Maislinger / p.192 Somm / p.193 Somm / p.194 Pion Studio / p.195 Pion Studio / pp.196 – 197 Pion Studio / p.198 Mövenpick Wein / p.199 Mövenpick Wein / pp.200 – 201 Mövenpick Wein / p.202 Cloud Wine / p.203 Kangkao Wine Club / p.204 Riedel Wine Bar & Cellar / p.205 Riedel Wine Bar & Cellar / p.206 Terroirs by LQV / p.207 Terroirs by LQV / pp. 208 – 209 Terroirs by LQV / p.210 Coupe de Vin / p.211 Coupe de Vin / pp. 212 -213 Coupe de Vin / p.214 Vetro & Enoteca / p.215 La Copa Oscura / pp.216 – 217 La Copa Oscura / p.218 Bar 81 / p.219 Pudao Wines / p.220 Graeme Kennedy / p.221 Graeme Kennedy / p.222 Park90 / p.223 RVLT / pp.224 – 225 RVLT / p.226 Goût de Jaune / p.227 Wineshop Flow / p.228 Apéro / p.229 Scotch Wine Bar / p.230 Lucinda / p.231 Dirk du Toit / p.232 Dirk du Toit / p.233 Dirk du Toit / p.234 City Wine Shop / p.235 City Wine Shop / pp.236 – 237 City Wine Shop / p.238 Dania Portman / p.239 Rob Palmer / pp.240 – 241 Rob Palmer / p.242 Vini Divini / p.243 Vini Divini / pp.244 – 245 Vini Divini / p.246 Nikki To / p.247 Noble Rot / p.248 The Puffin / p.249 The Puffin / pp. 250-251 The Puffin

In the same series

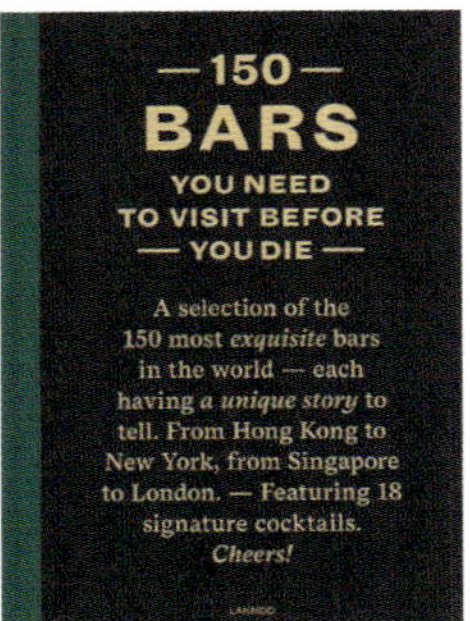

150 Bars You Need to
Visit Before You Die
ISBN 9789401486194

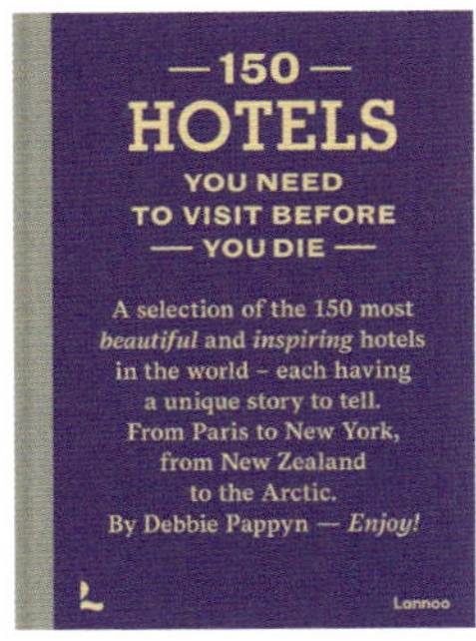

150 Hotels
You Need to Visit
Before You Die
ISBN 9789401458061

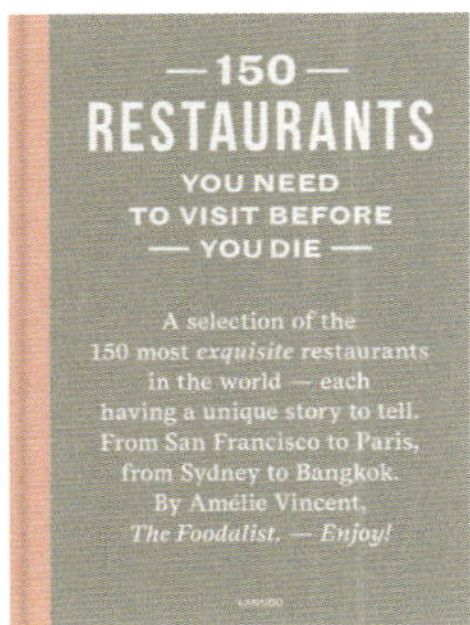

150 Restaurants
You Need to Visit
Before You Die
ISBN 9789401454421

150 Houses
You Need to Visit
Before You Die
ISBN 9789401462044

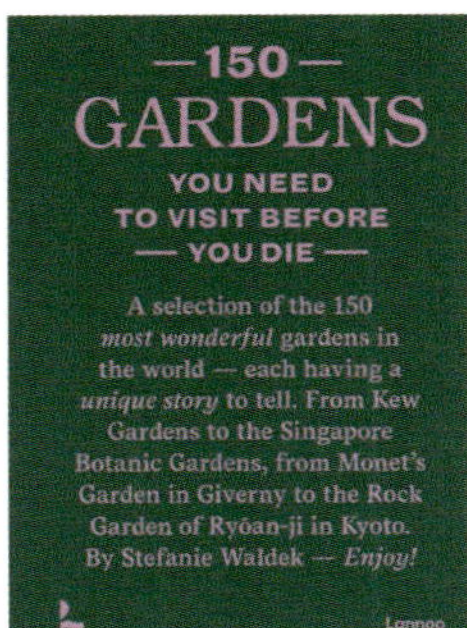

150 Gardens You Need
to Visit Before You Die
ISBN 9789401479295

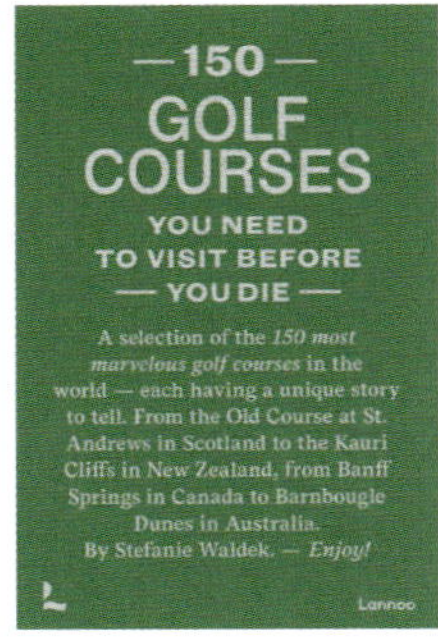

150 Golf Courses You
Need to Visit Before
You Die
ISBN 9789401481953

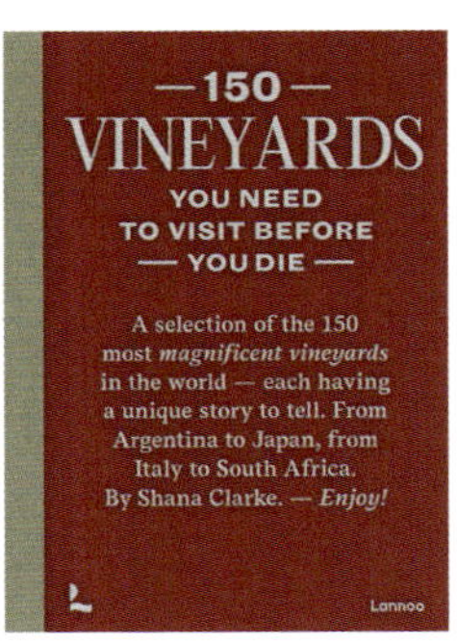

150 Vineyards
You Need to Visit
Before You Die
ISBN 9789401485463

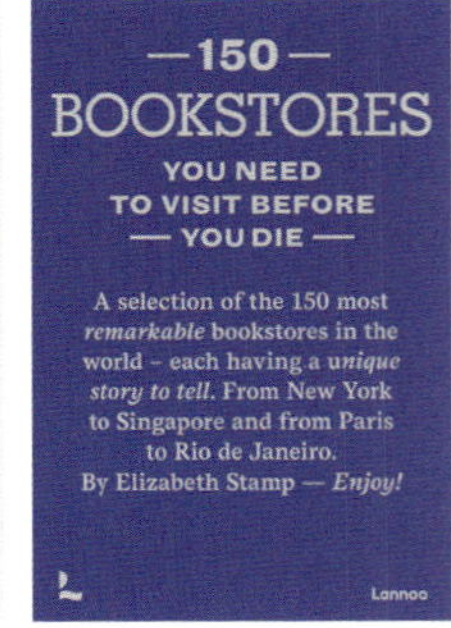

150 Bookstores
You Need to Visit
Before You Die
ISBN 978940148935 5

Colophon

Concept & selection
Jurgen Lijcops

Texts and photo selection
Léa Teuscher

Copy editing
Melanie Shapiro

Book design
ASB

Image back cover
The Puffin

www.lannoo.com

Sign up to our newsletter for updates on our latest publications on art, interior design, food & travel, photography and fashion, as well as exclusive offers and events.

If you have any questions or comments about the material in this book, please do not hesitate to contact our editorial team: art@lannoo.com

D/2023/45/478 - NUR: 440/500
ISBN 9789401486224